ART DECO MAN

The Legacy of John Gabriel Beckman

Roger Lee Kenvin

Edizione La Spiaggetta

Also by Roger Lee Kenvin

Long Run & Teatro Ruggiero

Trylons and Perispheres

After the Silver Age

The Cantabrigian Rowing Society's
Saturday Night Bash

Harpo's Garden

The Gaffer and Seven Fables

Krishnalight

With Verna Rudd Kenvin

Magellan Moon

Necessary Ports

ART DECO MAN

The Legacy of John Gabriel Beckman

Published by Edizione La Spiaggetta
8744 Shoshone Avenue
Northridge, CA 91325-3121

Copyright 2006 by Roger Lee Kenvin

First printing

Printed in Canada by Hignell Book Printing Ltd.

Library of Congress Control Number: 2003103885

ISBN 0-9656635-9-0

Acknowledgment

With thanks to all the people who contributed to this work, I would especially like to acknowledge the invaluable contributions by John and Louise Beckman, Jane Beckman, Grant Taylor, Patricia Anne Moore of the Catalina Island Museum, Ross Bellah of Columbia Pictures, Edward Zimmerman of Sony Pictures Television, and the staff of the Margaret Herrick Library of the Motion Picture Academy in Los Angeles.

Source materials are credited both in the text and in the notes at the end. Photographers for all photos are credited on their photographs. The front cover was photographed by the author. It depicts Beckman's Avalon murals as they appeared on two early postcards purchased at the Catalina Island Museum. This photograph is repeated in Appendix B in which other photographs of Beckman's murals in Catalina and the Chinese Theater appear. These photographs are also credited to the author.

For Jane, John, and Louise

Contents

Introduction

Everybody in the world is probably well aware of the collaborative nature of the theatrical arts. The credits rolled at the end of television shows or movies reveal the hundreds of talented people involved in every project. The star actors, a few charismatic directors or producers, though, are often the ones most remembered. The grips, gaffers, best boys, scriptwriters, musicians, set designers, costumers, although experts in their own specialties, are appreciated, but often only in the mass, not so much as individuals, except by those who work with them on a daily basis or on a particular film.

Four things attracted me to John Gabriel Beckman as the subject of a biography. First, he began working in movies in 1934, near the beginning of the golden age of sound, and, second, he never retired, still working at age ninety-one as Art Director for the television sitcom *Designing Women.* This means his career was extraordinary for its longevity and flexibility. Third, he was a person I first met in 1945 and resumed friendship with in the last years of his life. Not only was he a friend, but I admired him greatly as a man and a creative artist and felt others might like to know his story and his legacy. Fourth, his career was not limited to film and television, but also included two of Los Angeles' stellar attractions—the art deco murals in the Casino on Catalina Island and the decorations for the famous Chinese Theatre in Hollywood, perhaps the most recognizable theatre image in the world.

He was a gifted human being, hard-working, intelligent, personable, not unlike many who work in the film industry. Hollywood, so often and easily maligned, also includes many like John Gabriel Beckman, representing a pool of international creative people whose stories seldom get told. This book is a small attempt to honor all those who labor to provide the world with entertainment and enlightenment.

Roger Lee Kenvin

Sointula

His story begins in 1902 on Malcolm Island in Queen Charlotte Strait, British Columbia, in a community called Sointula, inhabited largely by Indians and a small colony of Finns. He is a slim, blond-haired boy of four who has noticed that the tide has gone out exposing rocks like miniature mountains, an oozy, spongy soil to dig one's toes into, and a horizon that seems wider than he has ever noticed before.

Overhead, the gulls scream and wheel in the sky, swooping down to crack clams on the rocks or snatch up small wiggling fish from the receding water. Clouds cross the anxious sky, with a downshaft of light from the sun occasionally spotlighting other pine-covered islands in the distance.

The boy feels the thrill of dangerous adventure, the romance of pushing alone into the unknown and uncertain. He climbs a rock and sits there for a long time, looking and thinking.

His name is John Gabriel Beckman, a child of Finnish background with mysterious Russian undertones. He has already finished his first painting, done at three and a half, of a pile driver in the Columbia River in Oregon. He has quickly developed a keen eye for details and for distant objects. He finds them intriguing. He has noticed the horses, the blue-grey skies, the ferryboats that lumber across from the mainland, the Indians who speak privately among one another and travel in canoes and fish so expertly.

What can be seen from this secure perch on the rock? Turn to the east, and maybe he could see across Malcolm Island to Echo Bay, Gilford Island and other islands crowned by the low mountains of the mainland beyond. Turn to the north, and he might imagine the icy wonders of Alaska, the north pole, and the possibility of a shimmering aurora borealis.

Turn to the west, and the town of Port NcNeill with the vastness of Vancouver Island behind it doesn't prevent one from knowing that the Pacific Ocean rolls out blue and booming all the way to a tiny China and Japan at its farthest reach.

Turn south, and one's gaze might meet Alert Bay, Beaver Cove, Telegraph Cove, and follow the serpentine strait as it becomes Johnston Strait and then melts into the Strait of Georgia beyond it. The architecture of the known world is a marvelous thing to behold when one is four years old.

But, suddenly, the gentle lapping below causes fear. Water all around, a flood that has silently crept in while one was musing. The young boy, frightened, calls for help. Luckily, his voice is heard. A man informs his father, a powerful 245-pound physician who wades in, swims out, tells his son to hold on around his neck, and brings him back safely to shore.

It is one of several early memories John Beckman has of life in Sointula. He remembers going with his father to an Indian sweat lodge. "I remember my father taking me to a long house with a dirt floor. Once a year they put on a spectacle in which they dug a long trench down the center of the house. In the evening, in the loin cloths they wore, they walked on the hot coals they had placed in the trench. It was so hot in there. It was as though you were in an oven. The smell was colossal. The Indians would talk among themselves. We stayed about fifteen minutes, and then left. Our clothes were soaked. It was some sort of ritual to them."

John Jr. reports, "There is a reconstructed long house there now with masks all around the inside perimeter, where visitors can walk right up and see all these items first hand."

John Gabriel Beckman also remembered going with the Indians at Christmas when they escorted him and his father to Alert Bay. Two Indians seated them in a dugout. They went to visit a chief whose son was born the same day John Beckman was, March 27, 1898. "We were both four years old. We exchanged presents. The boy gave me a little monkey on a string. When you pulled the string, the monkey climbed up."

Years later, at ninety years of age, John Beckman revisited Sointula in July, staying with Finnish relatives who listened and swapped stories. Beckman remembered his first medical emergency. "I cut off my thumb on a cross-cut saw. My father sewed it up, but when it's cold, it turns all white."

This man, so reserved and interior, who became one of Hollywood's leading art directors in films summed up the early years in Sointula: "I remember being alone so much of the time so that I wandered, as I did the rest of my life. I love to go places." His relatives and friends tried to help him reconstruct his past in Sointula. His son said, "They were most interested in having him tape his early memories. After we left there and drove down to Victoria, the local natives carved out a canoe from a whole tree trunk, as had been their custom, and John Beckman paddled with the natives quite expertly."

Mostly, Beckman remembered various celebrations and picnics from the Sointula years. "My father was in constant demand because he was a doctor. The Indians let him sit in their canoes, and he'd lie on his back because he was a big man and might have tipped over the canoe, and so he would look up at the sky. He took me with him sometimes. I remember an Indian with a shotgun who picked off a goat high on an island. The goat fell into the ocean. They paddled furiously toward it, saying that it would only come up once and they had to scoop it up then. That would be all."

On June 27, 1902, Dr. Beckman was selected as Vice President and Manager of the Sointula colony. On July 4, at the end of the dock a pole was set up with a sign proclaiming the town as "Sointula." Dr. Beckman claimed this made him "the first artist in town."

Three entries in a journal give one a glimpse into the colonists' life on the island:

> Friday, July 4th, 1902. The most noticeable building was built last winter—a loghouse including kitchen and other rooms. Little further away from it was just recently built a big

hall, which is not yet decorated inside. In between these buildings are tents which bottom part was built by cedar wood. Downstairs was made into a large storage room and next to it a newspaper office. Doctor Beckman and Mr. Krikla lived there and they also had a writing table and writing set.

Friday, July 11th, 1902. For the hospital foundation, it was decided to ask Doctor Beckman to provide beds and other necessities from his own institution in Astoria, Oregon.

Doctor Beckman described the delightful way of the melting pot of the world and how each one of us had ended up in Sointula.

In this part of the world they say they have a week of spring, a couple of weeks of summer, a week of fall, and the rest is winter. It was a noble experiment for the Finns attempting a colonization project there in that long, languid, blue-and-grey landscape so reminiscent of Finland itself, only more Spartan. Everyone had to pitch in. Johanna Maria's sister, Elena, acted as post-mistress for the colony. She was there in 1893 because the historical society has a copy of the druggist's prescription book in which Dr. Oswald Beckman prescribed sedatives for her in that year.

It was a hard life for Dr. Beckman eking out a living for himself, his wife, and three children—John (born 1898), Johanna Maria (born 1900), and Margarethe Sophia (born 1902) in Sointula. He stuck it out for two years, until a fire in a Finnish meeting house on the island took the life of one of his valued partners, along with several others. In this meeting house there were apartments as well as the omnipresent Finnish sauna, the heat from which was channeled through ducts.

When the fire started, the main heating duct acted like a flue, thrusting the fire upward. Dr. Beckman escaped by walking down the stairs and tried to persuade others to follow, but some were afraid and were trapped in the building. The tragic death of his partner saddened Dr. Beckman. He lost his zest for work in Sointula and moved his family to Portland for six months while John was sent to a school run by Catholic nuns back in Victoria.

Finally, the family boarded a ship named *Columbia* to sail to San Francisco. John remembers that this was the first steamer ever to have air-conditioning. Dr. Beckman told his son he had done work for two years for nothing in Sointula, and now he was going to make it pay in San Francisco. The year was 1905.

Dr. Oswald Heribert Beckman had been born in 1851 under mysterious circumstances. The family legend has it that his mother, Amanda Olivia Ammondt, had been a lady-in-waiting at the court of the Russian Czar, Nicholas I, and that this woman had become pregnant, presumably by the Czar, and given birth to a son, Oswald, illegitimately.

She then married Knut Adolf Beckman, a Lutheran minister, who had been born in Jalasjarvi, Finland, October 29, 1821, and, allegedly, falsified the child's birthdate from 1848 to 1851 so that it would not seem she was connected to the Russian court. Knut Beckman preached in the church in Tottijarvi from 1861 until his death from typhus at Turku, Finland, on May 25, 1868.

John Beckman, Jr., who has made two visits to Finland visiting relatives and checking the family geneaology, owns a book which is a geneaology of Finland before 1850. Based on information in this book, it would seem as though there were other children born to Amanda before Oswald came along, although John Jr. has very little else about Amanda's early life. He is skeptical about the Amanda-Czar story, though. As he points out, his Finnish relatives all bear strong family resemblances to Knut, and many of them are descended from Knut's second wife. Amanda was his first wife.

Still, the legend persists: John Gabriel Beckman recalled being awakened one night in 1912 in Russia to meet someone who came to visit—the head of the Russian army, the Czar's uncle. And his daughter Jane still has in her possession that tantalizing passport with its admonition that John Gabriel Beckman "be acccorded all the rights and privileges of the Russian royal family."

About Oswald Beckman, we also know that at an early age, probably about 1862, both he and his brother, Otfried, went to sea, Oswald as a ship's cook and the brother as a rigger. In the North Sea, the brother was lost while doing sails in the rigging. It was a bitter loss for Oswald.

He had many other adventures at sea, including a real disaster when his ship was sunk off Cape Hatteras, North Carolina, near the end of the Civil War. It took about two or three days for the ship to break apart, affording the crew time enough to get the cargo off the ship and make rafts to ride out the storm.

Oswald reached shore behind the Confederate lines in the south, and somehow, when he was sixteen, made his way north across Union lines by tagging along with a messenger to Boston. Allegedly, he shipped out of Boston for several years on a banana boat to South America, got stuck in Dutch Guiana for six months, and so quit the sea-faring life at twenty-four.

Apparently in the period from 1864-1872, he married his first wife in Boston, moved to Philadelphia, and got a job as orderly in a hospital. His son, Adolph, was born in November, 1879.

John Beckman used to enjoy telling this story of his sea-faring father, adding that his father had a private bank account in Portland where money would arrive regularly from Russia during his lifetime, thus affording his father the assurance of a steady income, and backing up the notion of those in the family that he may indeed have been the natural son of the Czar.

But, again, these are stories enjoyable in the telling and hearing, although John Beckman Jr. suggests they don't always add up. He points out that if you take either 1848 or 1851 for Oswald's birthdate, this would have made Oswald far too young to have gone to sea, somewhere between eight and fifteen. And the Civil War was over in 1865.

John Jr. adds that another story his father told was that Oswald was an interpreter when the Czarovich came to the United States, but we have no evidence that the young Czarovich ever visited the United States in that period.

John Jr.'s guess on this question is that Oswald probably was on a British ship that foundered off Cape Hatteras and rowed ashore, finally making his way north to Philadelphia.

Jane Beckman's information about these events differs somewhat.

She remembers that Oswald supposedly had a cousin who was an opera singer in Europe, and she understood that in either 1875 or 1876 the Grand Duke Alexis, younger brother of the Czarovich, came to the United States to see the West and hunt buffalo, and Oswald Beckman is rumored to have been his translator. She adds that Oswald also was at the Centennial Exposition in 1876 and is said to have worked as translator for foreign dignitaries.

At any rate, the Philadelphia years were consequential ones for Oswald. An impressive man physically, he was possessed of a voice described as "tremendous" by his son. "When he whispered, you could hear him for a block." In Philadelphia, he got a job in a hospital, working first as an orderly cleaning out bed pans. Of course, the fact that he spoke Russian, Finnish, English, French, Italian, Armenian, Swedish, and knew Greek and Latin, was not lost on the hospital staff. Jane says he also was semi-conversant in Portuguese, German, and Danish.

The hospital authorities said they would finance Oswald for four years of Jefferson Medical College. But he had, in the meantime, met a charming Irish woman who persuaded him to join her church so that he could sing in the choir with his magnificent bass voice. The people in the choir were so impressed that they said they would send him to Milan, Italy, to become an opera singer.

Thinking it over, he realized he wanted to marry his Irish sweetheart and thought it wouldn't be fair to subject her to a strange country with a different language, so he decided to accept the medical school offer and settle down in Philadelphia.

He graduated from Jefferson Medical College in Philadelphia in 1879 and became an eye, ear, nose, and throat specialist, after having been, first, a male nurse.

In that year also, his Irish wife bore him a son, Carl Adolf Hjalmar (called "Dolph" by his descendants), who survived and several other children who didn't. She was a good deal younger than Oswald, and eventually died in childbirth. The story goes that she came from a very wealthy family, and that Oswald, with young Hjalmar in his arms, knocked on the door of her family's mansion after her death, only to be turned away huffily by the family butler. Jane Beckman has some of Dr. Oswald's patients' records from the Philadelphia practice.

Oswald tried raising the son with a succession of housekeepers, and, according to his son, John, spent fifteen years in Philadelphia. Jane Beckman was told that, during his time in Philadelphia, Oswald assisted the doctor officiating at the execution of Charles J. Guiteau, the assassin of President James Garfield, in 1881, and helped perform the autopsy on his body afterward. This may have been the first time the electric chair was used.

Apparently, sometime in the 1890s, Oswald went back to Finland where he delighted relatives with a bicycle he brought with him, quite a novelty at that time.

John Gabriel Beckman said his father eventually traveled around the world, visiting the Crimea, among other places, and emigrating west at the urging of a friend who had a gold mine in Alaska. Stopping off in Astoria, Oregon, in 1893 (Jane says 1892), Oswald met an enterprising Finnish woman, Johanna Maria Pernu, a nurse/midwife who had emigrated from Finland in 1883 (Jane, 1888), heard they had some Finns operating a fish cannery in Astoria, and had talked a local bank into building a two-storey Finnish maternity hospital and who apparently had very little trouble prevailing upon Dr. Beckman to join the staff.

In 1997, John Jr. and his wife visited this location and talked to a woman who said that hospital became a boarding house eventually. At any rate, Oswald married Johanna Maria, and in 1898, their son, John Gabriel Beckman was born. However, even this date is questionable. Daughter Jane has Oswald and Johanna's marriage license which gives the date of their marriage as 1899. But John was always given to understand that he was born in 1898, so that is the date we have to accept.

According to Jane, the family moved back to Astoria in 1904. Dr. Oswald had bought several pieces of property there (near Warrenton, according to John Jr.), which stayed in the family at least up to the Depression (to 1940, according to John Jr.)

In Astoria, the Beckmans lived in the Winthrop house, a few blocks away from their friends, the Flavels. Years later, Jane and John's aunt Johanna would recall her youth there, remembering a steep drop-off to the street below, where a child could land in the tops of trees. She also said that her brother, John, liked to climb out the attic window and walk along the ridgepole of the house, three floors up, to the consternation of his mother.

John also had a Noah's ark with animals that was his favorite toy at this time, perhaps a harbinger of things to come when, like a god, he could arrange and manage a world—even though the artificial one of selected images in a film—as he wished.

Apprentice to the World

After the quiet island setting of Sointula, the busy city of San Francisco opened many opportunities for the Beckmans when they arrived there in January 1905. True to his word, Dr. Beckman now had a Nob Hill clientele, including the wealthy banker Harry Crocker and his family, who would come to the doctor's office at the corner of Stockton and Geary.

John and his sisters reveled in their new prosperity in this bright, bustling city, John often accompanying his enterprising father when he made his rounds. "I enjoyed the year and four months in San Francisco," John said. "It was a fabulous place. I was just old enough to appreciate the place."

There were many new places to visit—museums, parks, the Flood mansion on Nob Hill—and exciting people who came to dinner. John said he couldn't remember a single dinner in San Francisco when they didn't have at least two or three guests to dinner. It must have been a vivacious scene, with Dr. Oswald holding court. "Nobody would talk but my father," said John. Dr. Oswald mesmerized his audiences with his extraordinary seafaring stories and medical experiences.

The Beckman family apparently never lacked for servants in their new home, either. Jane Beckman said, "The invisible servants were never mentioned by father, but by Johanna frequently. They always seemed to be shirttail relatives of some sort that our grandfather was helping get started in America. Father took them for granted as part of the furniture, I guess. If you pointed at a photo and said, 'Who's that?' he'd say, 'Oh, that was our second cousin so-and-so, who was our cook' or housekeeper, or maid, or whatever."

But a new event was soon to change all their lives.

On April 16, 1906, John went with his father and five other doctors to the opulent Palace Hotel to have lunch with the famous Italian tenor Enrico Caruso who was appearing with the San Francisco Opera. Then, on April 17, John, with his mother and sisters, sailed on a lumber boat up to Mendocino County to visit friends in Ft. Bragg, leaving Dr. Oswald behind in San Francisco to attend to his practice. They landed at the dock and had to take a breeches buoy over to land where they registered at the local hotel.

The next day, April 18, the earthquake struck at 5:13 a.m., but the Beckmans in Ft. Bragg felt it first as it moved down the coast toward San Francisco. It devastated Ft. Bragg, moving the earth twenty-two feet. John knew something disastrous was taking place when he felt his bed slide from one side of the room to the other in the hotel.

Meanwhile, in San Francisco, Dr. Beckman had an early morning call and had left his home off Van Ness Boulevard to go to his office. Although he survived the quake, the home he left behind him went up in fire, and both his office, with his strongbox and records, and his bank nearby had to be dynamited.

For two days, fires raged throughout San Francisco. When it was over, five hundred and three people were dead and the damage amounted to three hundred and five million dollars. It was at this point that his bank changed its name from the Bank of Italy to the Bank of America so that it wouldn't have to honor Bank of Italy requests anymore.

Dr. Beckman and Elena helped take care of victims of the disaster. But the horror for the Ft. Bragg Beckmans was that for two weeks they didn't know whether Dr. Beckman was alive or dead. Communication lines were down, and so it was an especially joyful time when the family was finally reunited.

Jane Beckman's recollection of this period differs somewhat:

"Relative to the earthquake/fire, Dr. Oswald was not at his office, but went there directly. On the way, he bought a small wagon off a Chinese laundryman and loaded his instruments and records into it. The National Guard took it away from him, and dumped his stuff into the street. He must have managed to transport the stuff somehow, though, as I have his records, including his April 1906 rent receipt for his offices.

"The problem with the bank was that he didn't trust banks, so he kept all of his money in cash in a safe deposit box. It was NOT the Bank of Italy. They dynamited the bank and blew up the vault, which ruptured, and then the fire burned everything up. He was left with $200 in his pocket with which to start again. (Father said Dr. Beckman always carried several hundred dollars in cash with him at all times), Giannini saved the contents of the vault of the Bank of Italy (and, rumor has it, several other safes that didn't belong to him)."

With nothing left for him now in San Francisco, Dr. Oswald Beckman and his family soon moved to Ft. Bragg where Oswald resumed his practice. He wrote to classmates who lent him money to get started again. His brother, Adolph, was a pharmacist who could help. The Finns were very conscientious about helping one another in adversity.

John Gabriel said of his father, "He was a fantastic man. He was a man of great power, physically and mentally." Ft. Bragg now became the place that the young John Beckman lived out his formative years.

In 1910, however, Dr. Oswald, considering his young son's destiny, decided that the boy would do well with architecture as a career. He decided to send young John, along with aunt Elena, on a long voyage to Europe where the destination would be St. Petersburg in Russia where the boy would be enrolled in an architecture school. His 1910 passport, still in the possession of his daughter Jane, reads "to be accorded all the rights and privileges of the Russian royal family," further fortifying the idea of a significant Russian connection.

With his aunt, he traveled extensively throughout northern Europe for the next two years—to England, Ireland, Scotland, Sweden, Finland, Denmark, France, including a two-week stay in Paris where the wide-eyed student met all the current artists, including Claude Monet who painted huge canvases of water lilies and had a studio that also housed six to twelve other artists. John had a cousin studying art at the Ecole des Beaux Artes who taught him the basics of oil painting and gave him entree to this astonishing world of art. John later realized that he must have met at that time all the brilliant young artists who later became so famous throughout the art world. He remembers circulating from one fascinating studio to another. John later regretted he hadn't been four or five years older at this period in his life.

St. Petersburg, in contrast, was a disappointment. The directors of the school said a boy of twelve, no matter how talented or interested, was simply too young to enter the school. "Come back in two years," they said. Young John was willing, but continued his studies in Copenhagen instead.

After he had been away two years, his mother was alarmed at hearing rumors of the possibility of war breaking out. She also became ill at the same time, prompting John and Elena to book passage on a new ship sailing from Southampton in the spring of 1912, the *Titanic*. But because of the seriousness of Mrs. Beckman's illness, Dr. Beckman urged them to turn in the tickets and sail instead on a ship leaving earlier, the *Olympic*, which they did, thus averting the horrible fate that befell the passengers and crew on the *Titanic* on April 14-15, 1912.

The crossing on the *Olympic* was not uneventful. John remembered following the captain around, intrigued with the business of running a ship, and he remembered seeing icebergs in the north Atlantic and the powerful storm they ran into off the coast of Ireland.

One might have thought that back home again in Ft. Bragg, life would have seemed perhaps a little too tame for the young adventurer, but John's recollections of his adolescent years there show that he was really a pioneer California beach boy, surfing up the coast near his home about a mile above town. John remembered thirty-foot waves crashing against the cliffs, recalling fondly the planks he and a friend used as surf boards, even daring to sample danger during fierce winter storms. Underneath his quiet demeanor, John Beckman sometimes had a daredevil's heart.

In high school, he continued his art work. In his senior year he was editor of the Ft. Bragg Union High School Annual. There is a photo of him sitting proudly with his fellow students at a desk. He also supplied line drawings for the Annual during his last two years in school.

In addition, he worked on the local newspaper in town, eventually running the linotype machine for it. He was what was called a printer's devil. Years later, when his daughter Jane was a student at Cal Poly State University in San Luis Obispo, she took him to the university's printing shop museum, and he showed her how to run the old presses and equipment displayed there. Jane has notebooks in which her father designed airplanes and John Jr. remembers the turbine engines his father designed during the depression years.

A story the Beckman family loves to tell comes from this period. Dr. Oswald had a horse and buggy which he kept in a livery stable. John Gabriel was out riding in it one day. An automobile came by at a fast speed, spooking the horse which tossed out John Gabriel from the buggy. The horse returned to the stable by itself. With John Gabriel now sprawled out on the ground, another automobile came by, and a man said, "Can I help you? Are you hurt?" The man gave Beckman a lift back to the livery stable where John Gabriel said, "My father would like to thank you, I'm sure." So the two men went to Dr. Oswald's house where the grateful father asked the stranger, "Will you stay for dinner?" The man did, and it turned out he was Jack London, destined to become California's most famous writer.

Another story from this period the Beckman family, with their love of cars, enjoys telling involves Dr. Oswald, who, in 1914, had a two-seater Mercury Cycle, one in front of the other, on a wooden frame. This was a present for John Gabriel's sixteenth birthday. The family has photos showing him in the car with his cap's visor turned backward. Somehow it backfired and caught fire. He got a nearby farmer to help patch it up where the frame had burned. They took the contraption to a blacksmith shop where a metal strap was used to reinforce it. Dr. Oswald himself never drove, but had gotten his first car, a Chevrolet in 1915, and had a chauffeur who used to pick him up and take him wherever he wanted to go.

One more image from this period: John Gabriel Beckman alone with his father in a horse and buggy on a road in the redwoods. A forest fire breaks out. The danger of sudden panic. Dr. Oswald gets out, puts his coat over the horse's head, leads him and John out of the woods to safety.

Growing up as he did in Mendocino County, John always liked the outdoors. He enjoyed fishing and climbing in the mountains. His son relates, "One time when I was a small baby, he went up in the mountains with a friend, camped out, and put up a tent without a floor. Unknown to them, they had pitched their tent directly over a snakepit full of rattlers. In the night, the rattlers came out to hunt and the frightened men had to lie perfectly still for a long time until day broke again and the snakes left."

Another camping story from a later date has John, Layne and their daughter, Jane, camping in a 1953 Ford Station wagon. Layne heard a noise in the dark, shone her flashlight on the window, and on the other side of the glass was the nose of a bear.

John Jr. also cites another camping story to illustrate the tougher, more courageous side of his father people seldom saw. John and Layne were somehow in a stream bed when a menacing looking man came along on horseback. The glint of sunlight just then caught the brilliance of Layne's 3 1/2 carat emerald cut diamond engagement ring. He advanced in a threatening manner until John reached down, grabbed a handful of gravel, and said," You think you can do anything you want, but if you do, there will be sand in your horse's eyes." The man retreated and left the couple alone.

In 1915, at seventeen, John Gabriel Beckman graduated from Ft. Bragg Union High School, and was ready to tackle university studies. He could have gone to Harvard on a scholarship, but he lacked Latin, so he couldn't accept it. Instead, he went to the

University of California at Berkeley in 1917, but, oddly enough, he was now too independent to fit into the academic milieu. Perhaps he was also a little immature, suffering from his early experience with strict nuns as teachers.

"I didn't like Berkeley, and they didn't like me," John would say, explaining away this period. But, when pressed, he would also tell stories of how he argued with his French professor who, unreasonably, according to John, wanted to conduct the class in French, and his teacher in art class whom he mimicked and made fun of behind his back. His habit was to follow the art professor around while he was critiquing students' work, and then John would offer his own inimitable critique.

According to Jane Beckman, the teacher told her errant pupil to go out and draw the statues in the Hall of Sculpture. Instead, he drew caricatures of the statues, and so got dropped from class. The teacher dismissed him, but later called him on the telephone when he was getting an art exhibit ready, asking John if he would assist him in his efforts.

At Berkeley, John was also enrolled in R.O.T.C. since the United States was about to enter World War I. After being dropped by his art teacher, the R.O.T.C. was all he had left. His assignment was in the Army Air Corps where he trained on jennies. At this period he was living with his brother and his wife on Castro Street.

One day John Gabriel went to join his unit which was preparing to go overseas, ran for a streetcar, crossed over a lawn where he tripped and cut his leg severely on a protruding sprinkler, so badly that he had to be hospitalized.

When he finally was released from the hospital, the war was over. At any rate, his brief academic career at Berkeley misfired, which was a pity, because, had he applied himself, he would have added a wealth of information and learning to his natural talents and abilities.

It sometimes seems a particular irony in his life that, although he bristled at Berkeley's strictures, he later worked for over twenty-five years at Warner Brothers in Burbank, a studio that was run by Jack and Harry Warner as a very tight ship, in which even stars like Bette Davis and Humphrey Bogart had to punch time clocks to account for their time.

Now that he had declared his independence, he had to earn a living. His sister-in-law's sister, Jenny, worked for Contra Costa County's district attorney, Earl Warren, who may have been the one suggesting that John take a job in a shipyard where he put things together with rivets. Those who worked there were quite skilled in the technique of flipping hot rivets up in the air like pancakes which would be caught in cups by workers above, but one day, a man missed and the hot rivet dropped, killing the man who had sent it up. That was the end of John Beckman's career as a shipyard worker.

Another job he held in his post-college years was with the Hercules Powder Company working with explosive powder.

Sometime in this period also, he got a job in the experimental unit of Spreckels Sugar Company that manufactured the processing used for extracting sugar from beets. He loved this work. Later in life, a year or two before his death, he told his son and daughter-in-law that's what he really would like to have done in life.

He was fascinated by the science of things, of learning what made things tick. He enjoyed inventing things. His son reported that, when John had time during the depression, he made plaster of paris models of a turbine engine he was designing. On the lid of a cigar box he arranged the drawings he had made with cut-outs from illustration board that would show some of the parts.

He also was intrigued by astronomy all his life. Louise and John Beckman, Jr., have often spoken of the father's attraction to machines and automobiles, an interest shared by the son. Clearly, John Beckman's interests were far broader than the career he actually pursued.

But Beckman greatly respected his father's wishes and knew that he wanted him to choose architecture. It was entirely natural then that he turned to the very career his father had appointed for him. He took a job in a redwood tank manufacturing company, working in the architectural department.

In 1919, he worked for one year in Sacramento, for an architect named Selen, learning the trade. His friend, Harry Hall, had contacted him, telling of an opening in the firm. John's beginning there was memorable: He reported for work with a smart alligator valise in which he had put all his worldly possessions, including all his money. It was stolen, and so for several days, all he had to eat was one orange, until he received his first pay check. Among the projects he worked on that initial year was a courthouse in Marysville.

Then, in the following year, 1920, Harry Hall, who had in the meantime left Selen and gone to Los Angeles, wrote John a letter telling him that things were booming in L.A. "They're building more theatres. Come on down." Hall's letter persuaded John to turn his sights south toward the sunny city just beginning to rival San Francisco as a cosmopolitan center with the rise of the film industry there. Perhaps a man of John Beckman's background and talents could find great expectations among the creative mix in this new place called Hollywood.

Los Angeles

John Beckman arrived in Los Angeles in 1920. He was twenty-two years old, a tall, rangy man with a quiet, easy elegance about him and a taste for style in his clothing. Sophisticated and charming, he easily won friends, especially women, who were readily beguiled by his gallantry toward them.

He would soon go on a memorable Sierra Club outing at which a pretty brown-eyed young woman named Nellie Cahill from Farmington, Iowa, would mistake him for another man, waving at him in what seemed a flirtatious manner, causing him to notice her, which he did with the greatest of pleasure. He promptly asked her for a date which she just as quickly accepted—although not without some later regrets.

What she didn't know was that John was in the process of assembling a car, a 1914 Parton Palmer, which he had bought from a doctor. The car was a four-cylinder two-seater with no floorboards, no windshield, and no roof.

Arriving at the Clark House, a residence for single young women, where Nellie lived, she watched askance from the second floor as this strange contraption pulled up to take her on a junket to San Diego. She later said "I almost didn't come downstairs," but she did.

On the road to San Diego, the radiator cap shot back hot water onto the couple, and, then, on the return trip, the car burned out a bearing in San Bernardino, forcing the young couple to take the red car public transportation line back to L.A.

An interesting footnote is that in 1995-96 the Clark House for Single Young Women still existed in Los Angeles.

In 1923 John and Nellie would marry on Labor Day, just at the outset of his budding career in Hollywood. For their marriage, they drove with

Raymond Kennedy, the designer of both the Egyptian and Chinese Theatres in Hollywood, and his wife, to Santa Barbara, where they were married by a justice of the peace. Nellie giggled all through the ceremony, proving that love and humor are an irresistible combination. The Beckmans honeymooned at Samarkand in Montecito. At that time John was making $75 a week, which was a good amount. In four and a half years, he would be making $300 a week.

Los Angeles was good for John and he was good for it. Soon other members of his family arrived. Johanna and Margarethe, called "Greta," first, both of whom enrolled in art school. Greta apparently had a romantic interest in Ft. Bragg and wanted to work there, but Dr. Oswald said, "No daughter of mine is going to go to work." So art school in Los Angeles was deemed suitable for both daughters.

Then, Dr. Oswald and his wife arrived in Los Angeles for a visit. But Dr. Oswald had had a stroke in 1921 and died in 1924, ending the illustrious, dashing career of that indomitable man.

Dr. Oswald's grandchildren, John and Jane Beckman, cite an example of how family stories can become changed, depending upon who is telling and who is receiving. Jane had heard through her father that Dr. Oswald was given a gold nugget on a stickpin for his medical services in the Klondike. But John Jr. heard from Aunt Johanna that a miner had given it to Dr. Oswald on the occasion of the birth of his daughter, Johanna. John and Jane both conclude that Dr. Oswald told one story to his son, another to his daughter, and so, typically, with Beckman lore, always a little skepticism.

After Dr. Oswald's death, sadly, his son John dutifully went back up to Ft. Bragg, sold everything, lock, stock, and barrel, and took the cash and put it in a Los Angeles bank.

Then he looked around, bought a lot in Glendale, designed a single-frame construction house for it, studs and headers all exposed, a simple frame house, in which his sister Jo would live until her death in 1981. John Jr. recalls life there during several months in the depression years of the 1930s when the inhabitants of the tiny house included John, Nellie,

John Jr., the grandmother (now bedridden), her two sisters, John's two sisters, Jo and Margarethe, plus Nellie's mother. Shortly, the John Beckmans were able to trade a lot they owned in Venice for a nice apartment in Glendale, but everyone in the family felt the crunch of hard times in those years. With the Venice lot in mind, John Gabriel designed a house, probably the first house design he ever made.

John Jr. says he had a grand time in the Glendale house. He would put a Sousa march on the victrola and march around, carrying an American flag. He would also tip over a wicker chair, march up to it, and set it right again. John Jr. used to rise early before everybody else and go outside to play. One memorable day he sat on an anthill with red ants.

He also recalls a Northern California trip in 1936 for ten days, and an earlier one to Carpinteria in 1934 where they stayed at the Palace Hotel. There were fireworks at the beach, Roman candles, rockets, pinwheels on sticks in the sand, a wonderful time, as he remembers it.

But he also experienced the great tensions in the Glendale house. Nellie and Johanna were at loggerheads. Margarethe went to the State hospital because of this, although her problems predated this. Dr. Oswald, of course, had suffered a stroke and died. His wife had to be turned in bed regularly. There were just too many people in a four-room house for it to be truly comfortable for anyone.

Nellie had to make a lot of sacrifices in this period. Instead of an engagement ring, John had given her lots in Venice Beach. She now traded these lots for an apartment. Nellie chauffered the apartment house owner for some extra compensation. John Jr. remembers going along with her in their car which was a Packard sedan from the 1920s.

John Jr. has some other memories of the early 1930s: "In 1932 Johanna had a Studebaker roadster. On rare occasions, Dad would use it. I remember going with him to the Oak Knoll district of Pasadena where he did several interior designs. Years later in movies, he used some of those same interiors in location shots. In April, 1934, after going back to work for Meyer & Holler, Dad did two paintings in Yosemite over seven days. We stayed in a little cottage. There was a wood fire in a pot-bellied stove. You could hear bears at night opening up garbage pails. We drove up to Glacier Point the first day after the snowplows opened it up. The snow was as high as our car (a 1928 Lincoln). On the way home in the San Joaquin Valley, we heard a tire blow out. Then, two spare tires also blew out. That week at Yosemite was significant to me because it was the only trip my family really took until 1935 when we went to the Exposition in San Diego."

In Los Angeles, John signed on first with an architectural firm, Walker and Eisen, but soon worked with Gordon B. Kaufman, who had been a friend of Harry Hall, John's mentor.

From there, he moved to the firm of Meyer and Holler, staying put for some years and moving up the ladder to become Assistant to the Decorator and finally Decorator when the previous decorator moved on, sometime in 1922 or 1923. Mr. Meyer himself, John always said, was the best possible connection since he knew everybody in Los Angeles.

Meyer and Holler had built the showcase Egyptian Theatre (restored in 1999) in 1922 on Hollywood Boulevard, a stunning addition and a trend-setter for the Egyptian style, currently a craze in the film capital.

Meyer early recognized John's talent for painting, especially murals, which were much in vogue at this time. He didn't hesitate at all putting him in charge of the team designing the new Grauman's Chinese Theatre at 6925 Hollywood Boulevard, thus establishing John Gabriel Beckman as a dynamic new element in the art world of Los Angeles.

The theatre's murals were completed in 1927. John worked closely with his colleague, Raymond Kennedy, who was the designer of the theatre itself. Kennedy, a Princeton graduate, had won the *Prix de Rome* for his work in architecture and was famous for his design of the Egyptian Theatre.

John also worked on other theatres in the Los Angeles area—Anaheim, Long Beach, Fullerton—but particularly on the Mason Opera House in downtown L.A. where he inherited the decorator's job for *No, No*

Nanette, a hit musical when the head man quit. Beckman also designed the decorations for the Los Angeles National Bank Building. He soon discovered that his new employer, the Meyer and Holler firm, was a prestigious one, numbering among its alumni Harold Vail, an architect from San Diego; Leland Fuller, who later became a motion picture art director; William Wurster, also a set designer for films; and Berthold Gerrow, a well-known sculptor.

However, all was not perfect at Meyer & Holler. The chief draftsman, for instance, did some things John could not respect, like firing a man who got married, went on his honeymoon, leaving word where he could be reached.

As for Leland Fuller, one day Beckman said, "Leland, I understand you're bucking for so and so's job." Fuller blushed, but the next day, a simple notice was posted saying he would be Chief Draftsman. Fuller later became an architect and then an art director in films.

Grauman's Chinese Theatre had an artistic team of four working on it: The architect of the building, Raymond Kennedy; Walter Armstrong, who did the draperies; Berthold Gerrow, who did the sculptures; and John Gabriel Beckman, on the murals. They worked full-time on the theatre through 1925-1926 until the theatre opened on May 19, 1927 with the world premiere of Cecil B. DeMille's *King of Kings*.

Nellie always said she regretted missing the opening night, but she had a good excuse, since John Gabriel Beckman, Jr. was born on May 12, 1927, a week before the opening. Nellie also said the opening night was the only time the theatre used all the lights as designed by John Gabriel Beckman. Never again.

The Chinese Theatre is, perhaps, the world's most readily recognized theatre. Its distinctive green-and-red Chinese pagoda style with the thirty-foot tall dragon that sits over the entrance, its ruby red interior, oriental murals, brass and crystal pagodas flanking either side of the screen made it a wonder for all in the movie industry to behold. Sid Grauman, who owned the theatre, proclaimed it authentically Chinese. John Beckman said "the decision was made to do it in Italian Chinoiserie." Whatever its style, it set a certain tone with its exotic aura in a land where The Garden of Allah, The Brown Derby, the Chateau Marmont, and the Beverly Hills Hotel were bravely flaunting Hollywood's jaunty, sassy new architecture.

The Chinese Theatre gained further fame when, as legend has it, Norma Talmadge, accidentally stepped in some fresh cement in the forecourt, prompting her companions, Douglas Fairbanks and Mary Pickford to add theirs, thus starting a trend for footprints, handprints, even leg prints (Betty Grable), noseprints (Jimmy Durante), hoofprints (Trigger), bladeprints (Sonja Henie), and even profiles (John Barrymore). The Chinese Theatre, now owned by the Mann Theater Corporation, is visited by millions of people annually and has become a symbol of the Hollywood film industry to all the world.

John Jr. feels that his father really enjoyed himself most working on the Chinese Theatre. Beckman made trips up to Gumps in San Francisco, buying Chinese prints and *objets d'art* for the theatre. He also brought home a mandarin outfit for Nellie and appeared to be extremely happy, immersing himself in things Chinese. In the eyes of others in the industry, Beckman was now something of a specialist on Chinese decoration, and the Chinese style, like the Egyptian one, swept through Hollywood as the current rage. Beckman was in the right place at the right moment.

Beckman's murals cover most of the lobby area of the theatre. The main display on the large wall above the concessions is a series of vertical Chinese screens on a black background in which one views pagodas, tea houses, temples, massive flights of stairs, gardens with twisted tree trunks, boats on distant lakes, fawns, and people strolling, some as lovers hand in hand, others in rickshaws or on boats on tranquil ponds, or taking tea, or crossing bridges like the figures seen in Blue Willow china. It is a world that is meticulously executed, beautifully exotic and stylized—inviting, unusual, frozen forever in time.

The murals extend into every area of the lobby. Tall trees, the tops of pagodas, stylized trees with gold leaves cover even the side panels and the doors. The ceilings, the chandeliers, every detail in the Chinese Theatre are all part of the grand design. Gold, red, black, and light blues predominate. The overall effect is very pleasing and complete, offering an excursion into an Asian world that appears serene and beautiful.

The Kennedy, Beckman, Gerrow, Armstrong team created a movie palace of lasting interest, one of the great monuments of Los Angeles. Fortunately, the Mann Corporation, which now owns it, has taken reasonable care to maintain it properly, even though it has been added on to accommodate additional film screens. The theatre occupies the major portion of the Hollywood Boulevard block between Orange and Orchid Streets and is still used for major film premieres as well as daily showings.

John and Louise Beckman have the design for the ceiling of the Chinese Theatre and other drawings of that nature in their collection.

Aaron Betsky in an article *(Los Angeles Times,* November 7, 1991) on the architecture of the Chinese Theatre first berated it as "a piece of bad architecture. Nothing quite fits, nothing quite matches, and nothing quite makes sense." But he admits, "The theater succeeds because it combines the grandeur of a kind of imperial Shangri-La with the sense that when you enter, the city disappears."

It also succeeds because it makes sense in terms of its spaces. In between matching fronts, you enter into an elliptical courtyard where a covered walkway leads you into a lofty space whose verticality and curved walls remove you, without separating you from the life of the city. There, you are prepared for the grandeur of the movie theater, where marble columns soar up to misty vistas seemingly held up by giant beams and guarded by strange ogres, dragons, and saronged sages.

For the Sunday, May 15, 1927 *Los Angeles Times,*
Marquis Busby provided readers with a preview of the
opening night:

> Red is the dominant note of
> Chinese art, and it is in the many
> shades of this color that the
> Chinese Theater has been decorated.
> Red, shade of the Tanager's wing,
> the delicate tints of coral, ruby
> blood, crimson, scarlet, wine, every
> conceivable shading of this most
> brilliant color of the spectrum is
> found in the great auditorium.
> This, of course, is only the central
> note. Almost every color in the
> chromatic scale has been used. The
> colors are almost breath-takingly
> magnificent.
> But before the spectator enters the
> theater itself he must pass through
> a lovely oriental garden, an
> enormous elliptical forecourt with
> forty-foot walls. Here are full-grown
> cocoa palms, tropical trees and
> trailing verdure, for it was the
> custom of the Chinese to bring
> woodland life into the heart of their
> cities.
> An ornate pagoda garden house in
> this forecourt forms the box office.
> The bronze square cut pagoda roof,
> ninety feet above the forecourt, aged
> to the color of green jade, is
> underlaid by two immense piers of
> coral red. Beneath the piers is a
> great stone dragon, and in front of
> the dragon, a bronze statue
> symbolizes the human genius of
> poetry and drama, while sur-
> rounding golden flames suggest the
> ever-burning fires of dramatic fancy
> and creation.

Directly beneath this statue is the entrance to the main foyer of the theater. This main room is flanked on either side by smaller vestibules, brilliantly decorated in red lacquer, silver and gold.

The main auditorium, which seats 2220 on one floor, has been so designed, it is said, to suggest a shrine during the dynasty of Haia, when the world was very young indeed.

The walls of this great room are of red brick, with fanciful trailing leaves, birds and figures drawn in soft silver tones.

It is the center doily in the ceiling which will perhaps attract most attention when the brilliant first night audience sees the theater Wednesday. This is sixty feet in diameter, and is entwined with silver dragons in relief, bordered by a circle of gold medallions. Extending to the sidewalls are a myriad of panels, each presenting some fanciful scene of Chinese antiquity.

From the center of the doily is suspended a gigantic chandelier in the form of a colossal round lantern. This is unexpressively lovely with its trailing strands of tiny incandescent bulbs looking for all the world like a jewel of fabulous worth.

Out of the way places of the world were combed for furnishings of the theater. The rugs were woven in China after designs prepared to harmonize with the theater itself.

The auditorium rug is of flame color with a jade-green shade relieving the warmth. The length of the repeat in the design is the largest ever woven, it is said.

The chairs were especially designed, and are upholstered in red with flower designs on the seat backs.

Simulating the twin doors of a lacquered cabinet, the fireproof curtain of the stage depicts a mimic Chinese world against a peacock blue background.

The stage itself is the third largest in this country, being surpassed only by those in the New York Hippodrome and Los Angeles' Shrine Auditorium. The stage opening is 160 feet wide, 71 in height and 40 deep.

After he did the Grauman's Chinese Theatre, John's talent and success in painting encouraged him to strike out for himself, setting up as a decorator and painter of murals. He achieved considerable success and renown in this area, although he didn't always get every assignment he wanted. He submitted a design for the Pantages Theatre, for instance, but lost out to B. Marcus Priteca. Nellie said he lost because he didn't have enough commercial sense, meaning that making money was not his chief aim.

However, he still did well. In 1928 John and Nellie looked at their assets and discovered they now had $10,000 in the bank, a lot of money. John couldn't decide whether to take the family to Europe for cultural reasons or go into business for himself. Nellie was reluctant to expose her year-old baby to uncertainty at that time, and, besides, her mother had just been hit by a car and broken her wrist, and so John now wisely became a self-employed businessman, hiring artists like Emil Kosa, Count Oulianoff, Eugene de Goncz and others to work for him. He and Emil Kosa would often go out together painting *en plein air* at this time also. Kosa, like Beckman, would later become an art director for films.

Some of Beckman's self-employed assignments at this time and afterward included the Hamilton food chain, the Janss drug store in Westwood, a house or two in Pasadena for which he supplied the interior decoration, and a concert setting for a musician.

In 1931 he did the murals for the Christian Science Church on Central Avenue in Glendale. Later, he would do the interior decoration in the home of religious leader Aimee Semple McPherson, the occasion of a bitter disappointment since McPherson and her business manager, a Mr. Mullen, kept changing their minds, causing Beckman to undo his work without getting paid for it. He was at the mercy of their indecisive whims, and it didn't seem fair to John and Nellie.

After all, this was 1932, and at the end of 1930, with the depression in full sway, the Beckmans had lost both their house and car. In these years, John, along with Emil Kosa and Sam Johnson, to make ends meet, contracted to do 9" by 12" oil paintings set in little gold frames for Bullocks. The Beckmans were then living on Virgil place. With John Jr. in kindergarten, Nellie was managing the court there in return for free rent.

John Jr. recalls, "Dad, Kosa, and Johnson were cranking out miniatures. Moving out of their office space, they hired a truck with a hitch. Dad was loading when he was suddenly engulfed in a cloud of steam. A delivery truck had come up behind him and lost its brakes. The only thing that saved him was this hitch. He was in the middle of it."

Off and on during the succeeding years, John would take on independent projects. In 1945, for instance, he would design a nursery in the Summit Drive, Beverly Hills home for Charlie Chaplin and Oona O'Neill's daughter, Geraldine.

Particular friends of the Beckmans in the early years in Los Angeles were the Monaco family, especially the two brothers Dr. Rudolph and Armand. The family, originally from Italy, was very successful, and the two brothers shared the Beckmans' interest in automobiles. John Jr. likes to relate how a dealer ordered two Voisin Avion 1926 true coupe de villes, four-door convertibles in which the top comes up only to the back of the front seat. The film actor Rudolph Valentino purchased one, and the Beckman's friend Dr. Rudolph Monaco the other for $16,000. Rudolph's brother Armand kept the car on blocks until 1952 when he sold it, but all the Beckmans were greatly impressed with this exotic car while it lasted.

In 1925, Dr. Rudolph Monaco had saved John Gabriel Beckman's life when his appendix burst and peritonitis set in. Rudolph decided to do a spinal bloc in which John counted the seconds and Rudolph counted the minutes. Although John's life was spared. sadly, Dr. Rudolph Monaco died several years later from cancer of the spine.

In 1927, when Grauman's Chinese Theatre was finished and the public was still oohing and aahing about it, someone introduced John to David M. Renton, a building contractor from Pasadena, who told him about a new casino William Wrigley of chewing gum fame was planning to build in Avalon on Catalina Island. Renton was impressed with John's work and introduced him to Mr. Wrigley.

John had dinner with the Wrigleys at their spacious home on Orange Grove Boulevard in Pasadena (now headquarters for the Rose Bowl Tournament) and two days later John made a sketch of what he thought might be interesting in a theatre. This sketch got John the job. Mr. Wrigley was immediately impressed with John's concept.

It is easy to see why he was impressed. The sketch reveals one side of the theatre illuminated in an otherwise darkened auditorium. What one sees is a semicircle of imaginative shapes set on a light blue background.

The design is mostly a melange of various things. One discerns a ceiling with wheel-like spokes flaring out over a demi-heaven dome of angels, nymphs, illustrated trees, fanciful rosettes, and flowers, a stylized boat floating somewhere in a Venetian-Japanese lake, a garland of male masks, most of whom look like Russian anarchists, one of whom looks like Charlie Chaplin, a coat of arms strategically placed, showing what appears to be a Greek aulos-player with a dancing woman, a small island of Greek orthodox churches looking like a replica of Santorini, and lots of petroglyphic-like symbols suggestive of dreams, primitive religions, or feverish illustrations.

At the bottom right are several versions of stylized waves. The ceiling of the theatre itself, instead of stars, has rosettes and flower blossoms floating in its darkness.

William Wrigley could see clearly that he had an artist of uncommon vision, imagination, and popular appeal in John Gabriel Beckman.

Catalina

Santa Catalina Island is one of California's greatest treasures. A jewel set in the turquoise Pacific Ocean twenty-four miles off the coast of Los Angeles, Catalina is a mountainous island about twenty miles long and eight miles wide, with a Mediterranean climate, many charming coves and headlands, and only one small town, Avalon, set in a gorgeous protected crescent-shaped harbor. The island is 85% in its natural original state, rising to a height of 2,125 feet in Mount Orizaba, and, thanks to the Santa Catalina Island Conservancy, set up in 1975, it will forever stay that way.

Originally discovered by the Portuguese navigator Juan Rodriguez Cabrillo in 1542 and claimed for Spain, the island was subsequently owned by Mexico until it became part of California in 1848.

It owes its great popularity, however, to William Wrigley Jr., the chewing gum magnate and owner of the Chicago Cubs. The Wrigleys would leave their Chicago home to spend part of every year in Pasadena where they had purchased a part interest in Catalina Island, then owned by the Banning family. In 1919, Wrigley purchased the island outright, intending to develop it as a resort center. Three generations of Wrigleys—William Jr. (1861-1932), Philip K. (1894-1977) and grandson William Wrigley, have made the island one of California's premier places for boating enthusiasts, fishermen, hikers, bicyclists, and naturalists, as well as day-trippers who come over for a relaxing stretch of beach and sun in Avalon. The Wrigleys built up the glass-bottom boat industry, erected a dance pavilion, gave the island the Catalina Bird Park, a country club and golf course, and provided tourists with three ships—the *SS Avalon*, *SS Cabrillo*, and *SS Catalina* to bring people over from the mainland. Today, there is a Wrigley ranch high up on the island that offers Arabian horses and riding demonstrations, plus an airport heavily used by small planes.

The Wrigley family also gave the island other much-needed facilities such as a dam to assure an adequate water supply, a couple of mines to provide year-round employment, and several buildings designed in early California Spanish-type architecture to give the town of Avalon a romantic, pleasing appearance. Catalina tile, made on the island, has become a staple of the business life of the island, and is much seen everywhere in Avalon.

Another aspect of Catalina is that there are very few automobiles on it—only essential ones. Most people zap around in golf carts, bicycle, walk, or use the local bus. With a hilly, mountainous terrain, Catalina bears more of a resemblance to Capri than it does to Bermuda, but it still ranks with these islands as a beautiful, restful place to visit or live in. It looks for all the world like a wondrous Mediterranean isle blown in secretly at night by some imaginative storm. Avalon, a town of about two thousand permanent residents, sits on a picturesque quayside and extends up the mountains all around. At one end, on Sugar Loaf point, sits the new Casino, and it is at this juncture that our story picks up.

In 1928, William Wrigley Jr. wanted to build a new Casino. His son, Philip, suggested having a ballroom upstairs and a theatre down below. The term "casino" to them did not mean gambling—there never has been gambling in this building—but rather a place of social concourse where people could dance and listen to music in a glamorous setting.

The Sugar Loaf site had housed a Casino, built in 1920, but it could only accommodate two hundred and fifty dancing couples. Wrigley may have had something like the Casino at Monte Carlo in mind, since the setting on the harbor very strongly resembles the principality of Monaco, and, indeed, the current Casino at first glance could easily beguile one into thinking one is looking at Monte Carlo. Some advertisers have even used the Avalon casino as a Monte Carlo substitute in their quick, clever television commercials.

Wrigley wanted a very large ballroom for dancers, coinciding nicely with the rise of big bands, like Jan Garber, Dick Jurgens, Kay Kyser, Freddie Martin, Benny Goodman, all of whom, plus more, played in the Casino's ballroom. In 1929, the new ballroom held five thousand dancers. In 1979 it would be cut to two thousand. It is still used for elaborate parties, weddings, corporate banquets, etc., and has acquired an illustrious history with the many lives it has had, such as in World War II when the USO took over and brought in entertainers like Bob Hope, Alice Faye, and Kate Smith to entertain the servicemen who were stationed on the island.

The architectural firm of Webber and Spaulding was hired to execute Mr. Wrigley's plan, with the lion's share of the planning going to project architect, Rowland Crawford. The building has been variously described as being Moorish or Mediterranean in style. It doesn't really matter. Its eclecticism is the kind of appealing Romanticism one finds in so much of Southern California architecture. The upper balcony, for instance, that encircles the ballroom, is said to have been based on the Alhambra in Granada, but it doesn't really remind one of that beautiful place at all. The style is simply a generous blend of attractive elements made all the more beautiful by the gorgeous setting in Avalon's hemispherical harbor. The Casino, because of its strategic setting on a spit of land, is a focal point from any angle in the town of Avalon.

John Beckman's work on the Casino is divided into two areas—the exterior and the interior. On the exterior, just inside the loggia surrounding the main entrance, are nine panels that were supposed to have been executed in Catalina tiles, but were actually painted in fresco on the concrete surface itself in order to meet the opening deadline. Later, in 1986, one of the panels, featuring a mermaid, would be completed in tile by Richard Keit under Beckman's direction. The plan was to do the others in glazed tile, also, but as of 2006, this has not yet been accomplished. The restoration techniques used by Keit and Beckman were described by Steve Henson in the *Los Angeles Times Magazine*, January 25, 1987:

Creating tile glazes from scratch out of aluminum silicate and various combinations of metallic oxide was as much science as the original line drawing was art. Keit devised and tested about 6,000 glaze formulas to come up with the 163 colors in the 398-tile mural.

Meanwhile, Keit sketched the mural on paper at 40% of its actual size from an old two-inch, black-and-white photo that Beckman had provided. The drawing was enlarged to full scale and divided onto 12 silk-screens that were then used to transfer to the tile. After hand-applying the glazes with a bulb syringe, Keit fired 70 tiles at a time in his kiln, which is the size of a large vending machine. Materials cost $25,000, and Keit and Beckman donated their labor.

The finished product was critiqued carefully by Beckman, whose signature is inscribed above Keit's on the mural. 'Richard has done a magnificent job with the Art Deco detailing and with the mermaid,' he says. 'She was meant to be beautiful, and she had lost her charm. Certainly, there are a few details that I would have done differently, but I think it is a major work of art. It's jewelry, really.'

The exterior murals are various scenes of underwater life, perhaps inspired by Catalina's waters. Beckman had first visited the island in 1920, and, like many other visitors, had ridden in the glass-bottom boats to view undersea life in the clear waters. Eight of the panels have a watery green background with wavy white lines across the front simulating the motion of water, reinforced by bubbles rising to the surface.

Stylized marine life is seen, ranging from fan-like plants, feathery fronds, spindly-twigged branches, coral, squids with drooping tentacles, crayfish with long streamers, sea horses moving like a corps de ballet, conch shells, sea urchins, garibaldis, exquisitely arranged like polished jewels in the sea.

The central panel—the one now in tile—shows a tall Lalique-like mermaid, her red hair floating up toward the surface, a long, angular body, with her fish tail licking her thighs as though she's wearing an art deco stocking. She exists in a light blue-pink sea, flanked by three pink-and-blue sea horses and a trio of garibaldis.

On either side, magenta, pink, and blue frondy plants rise toward the surface, imitating the flow of her hair. One is struck by the geometry of the sea in all these murals, by the oriental stylization, the quiet, imaginative quality, and, above all, the serenity and the strength of the vision.

Because these exterior panels are exposed to the elements, they have had to be retouched over the years. This job has been done by Catalina artist Roger M. Upton, Sr., and his son, Roger M. Upton, Jr.

The interior murals, those in the Avalon Theatre itself, pose another problem. They are painted, not directly on the wall, but on a heavy jute material used to aid the acoustical qualities of the auditorium. As a result, this necessitated a different kind of painting technique and maintenance, neither particularly easy. Complicating the task was the fact that the jute is arranged in a series of triangles around the base of the wall and that dust has a tendency to collect in the seams.

Beckman used eleven different ground pigments, placing them in a medium of flatene so that they would stick to the jute. This has worked remarkably well, except that over the years, the colors have softened somewhat and the silver has lost a little of its original brilliance.

Beckman assembled at least five artists to work with him. Some had also worked with him on the Chinese Theatre. These men were Count Vyseled Ulianoff, Alexander Kiss, Emil Kosa, Jr., Eugene de Goncz, and Aloyous Bohnen.They did the actual painting from sketches prepared by John Beckman. In addition to the artists, other men helped them with their work. They often worked twelve to fifteen hours a day in order to bring the project in on schedule.

The effect, on entering the Avalon Theatre, is stunning in the completeness of the visual concept.

The fire curtain, an inverted semicircle, features a man looking ahead and his twin facing backward, standing on a huge stylized oriental wave in a sea of other waves.

Behind them is a topographical view of Catalina Island itself executed in gold leaf. These were originally described as being the flight of fancy westward, perhaps a bow to the patron, William Wrigley, Jr., himself, who had moved from Chicago to California, thus typifying the movement of many Americans westward.

Surrounding one in this predominantly red auditorium are the massive murals on the walls. On the left, there is a striking mural of a Spanish ship, sails highly stylized, sailing on a geometric sea toward a shore where a group of hooded friars wait in a land of huge flowers where birds soar downward through the skies like lethal dive bombers about to spring a surprise attack.

On the right wall, slim, elongated, naked native Americans charge with lances on sixteen-foot long flying horses in an exotic landscape of Oz-like proportions. Other unusual elements in the wrap-around murals are mountain goats jumping, graceful as gazelles, waterfalls, unusual birds, and exotic monkeys with black-and-white faces.

Above the proscenium arch of the theatre, the pipes of the organ converge in a grillwork arranged like overlapping clouds, in the center of which is a Botticelli-like Venus on a shell, rising from the sea, supported by Triton, Neptune, and sea horses.

Actually, the total effect of the murals with their pyramidal rising and falling around the theatre, gives the impression of the strength, power, and beauty of the sea around Catalina.

At the time the murals were painted, they were called futuristic. Some have also cited them as a good example of art deco, and they have also been described as art nouveau. Whatever they are, they are evocative, they appeal to all ages, and have a timeless storybook quality about them. One can read into them the history of California or the story of Catalina, if one wants to.

This might be a good place to consider the meaning of the terms "futurism," " art nouveau," and "art deco" since they have very specific connotations in the art world, and I have just used all three of them in discussing John Beckman's work. Whether any or all apply or do not is up to each person's intelligent consideration of Beckman's work. Labels are by their very nature slippery and imprecise, but it does not hurt to consider what they meant once.

Futurism was a movement in art and literature centered in Italy from about 1909 to 1916, although its influence continued in the art world and ultimately made its way into cinema.

A central tenet was that artists and writers should express the vortex of modern life, particularly through steel, fever, pride, and headlong speed. This means that the machine and its world should be glorified—speed, motion, dynamism. The futurists felt that if you painted a train, an airplane, a horse, or a human being, you should show it in flight, not with just four legs, if it were an animal, but with many legs, expressed as a triangular shape hurtling through space.

The artist, Umberto Boccioni (1882-1916) was a leading exponent of this style and wrote a *Manifesto of Futuristic Painters* which was presented to a large audience in Turin in March, 1910.

This document says that all things move, run, change their shapes rapidly, and that this dynamic quality, this vortex of motion, is what artists should strive to represent.

Since John Beckman was in Europe in this year, it is possible that he came into contact with futurism or had hints of its existence, but generally, he was not a devotee of machines in motion in his art work, only in his private life.

More likely, this term meant, to the people who used it about Beckman's work, the rather loosely expressed idea that his work presaged a future world of clean-cut, utilitarian peace, harmony, and unity, or some such, an imprecise usage with no particular reference to the strict European artists' idea of Futurism, but more closely related to the term "streamlined" as it was used in 1930s' America about automobiles, airplanes, and the New York World's Fair of 1939.

Art Nouveau, on the other hand, was a French term from the nineteenth century referring to a style or an attitude that showed up primarily in architecture, interior decoration, and graphics.

It included a decorative element, a pre-disposition criticized by the great painter Paul Cezanne as being extraneous. He referred to Paul Gauguin, for instance, as "a maker of Chinese images," derisively dismissing that current interest in the Oriental arts which had cropped up in the west after the opening up of Japan in the nineteenth century.

There had been a corresponding interest in the decorative arts in Great Britain called the arts and crafts movement, initiated by William Morris who produced furniture, wall paper, illustrations, and tapestries.

All these elements created an appreciation for decoration for decoration's sake, a mannered attitude that came to be known as art nouveau. Connoisseurs of the work of Rene Lalique (1860-1945) in jewelry and crystal, and Louis Tiffany (1848-1933) in glass, well understand the correct meaning of art nouveau.

Art deco also had its origin in France in 1925 when the *Exposition Internationale des Arts Decoratifs et Industriels* was held in Paris. This might be seen as a logical outgrowth of art nouveau, but it advocated a stronger emphasis on geometric shapes, bold outlines, jazzy shapes, and new elements from industry.

The jute that John Beckman used for the Avalon Theatre murals, for instance, was an unusual medium for an artist to choose, and the geometric shapes found so often in his flowers and figures are also characteristic of this style. Many art deco products were made of new materials like glass, plastic, metal.

For examples of Art Deco, one thinks of the Chrysler Building in New York, for instance, or the classy backgrounds in the Ginger Rogers-Fred Astaire movies. In the 1930s, the streamlined trains, cars, planes, furniture one saw often exhibited an artistry in their basic materials and in their total effect.

Because of the highly decorative element in John Beckman's work on the Chinese Theatre, the theatre and casino at Avalon, the umbrella term "art deco" seems appropriate for his work.

Beckman said about his work on the Catalina murals:

> On the Casino, the concept was mine. Then we did the preparation, execution, and painting. I would set the color scheme and style, then they would do the execution of the walls, ceilings, burlap, etc. I would do portions of them and test to see if they would work. From my sketches, they would prepare the drawings on paper, then charcoal or chalk them on the walls. Artists are touchy. They feel they are part of it and doing just as much as I am. And they are right. I love activity.
>
> These men had worked with me on the Chinese Theatre. Ulio did hands and faces. Emil Kosa had done Italian interiors. He was very versatile. I was flexible with style, always changing things.
>
> The whole concept of the theatre interior was to make it gay, pleasant, modern, with a certain lightness, airiness.

During the winter of 1928, John Beckman stayed at the St. Catherine and Atwater hotels. He had an office on the second floor of the St. Catherine hotel. Since it was his practice to go for a swim every morning, he noticed that usually someone on the balcony would wave at him—probably because very few hardy souls dared brave the cold Pacific during the winter, even at Catalina. But they didn't reckon with Beckman and his intrepid Finnish stoicism.

Occasionally, William Wrigley, Jr. would drop in to see how he was doing.

"I liked him very much," Beckman said. "He was open-minded, open-hearted. He did everything for Catalina. He built the casino with the theatre so the local people would have something to do. He promoted work for the people who lived on the island."

Beckman also had high praise for the engineer, D. M. Renton: "He was a fine man. He wanted everything done well and on time."

For the ballroom in the casino, Beckman provided the color scheme. A local man, N.A. Walburg supervised the actual work, which was done by Catalina people.

The ballroom is an impressive room, enhanced by concealed lighting which plays over a very large dance floor, about ten thousand square feet. The ceiling, fixtures, wall panels are all executed in a restrained, tasteful art deco style. The room is used today mostly for large functions like weddings and conferences, but also for concerts.

Its heyday, of course, was during the 1940s, including the war years, when big bands like Sammy Kaye, Jan Garber, Freddie Martin, Glenn Miller, and Benny Goodman played there.

Alcoholic beverages were never served, of course, so an enormous soda fountain was eventually installed, and there never was any gambling in the building.

John Beckman returned to the island in 1978 just prior to the fiftieth anniversary of the casino and remarked, "Catalina in 1929 was a fantastic place, but now there is more life, more activity. I think the atmosphere and the air is so beautiful. Catalina still retains a certain atmosphere and feel about it."

He also returned to the island in 1986 when Richard Keit re-did the Mermaid mural in glazed tiles.

Beckman's memory is permanently enshrined in the Catalina Island Museum, housed in the casino, where a copy of his contract with the Santa Catalina

Island Company is on view, along with other Beckman memorabilia, including some of his original drawings for the murals. The excellent small museum also contains valuable resources about the building of the casino and the island in general.

The contract reveals that Beckman had estimated the cost of the project to be $12,000 for the theatre and $900 for the asbestos curtain. The Santa Catalina Island Company agreed to furnish all labor, material, and other expenses, with all labor and selection of materials to be under Beckman's supervision.

He was paid $30 a day plus an allowance for room and board. The Company also paid him a 10% bonus upon completion of the project. It seems like very little today, but that was a really substantial amount of money in those days.

On February 24, 1929, when the Casino was nearing completion, the *Los Angeles Times* ran an article telling readers what to expect:

> The Catalina theater building is of circular type of enormous size. A total of 10,000 sacks of cement was required for the concrete work; 1500 tons of structural steel for 28,222 separate pieces for braces; 422 tons of reinforcing steel and 25,000 yards of sand and rock for the foundations. The roof requires 105,000 Catalina redcurved tile. The theater auditorium, on the main floor, is 115 feet in diameter. The full dome ceiling is forty-five feet high and the theater will seat 2500 persons.
>
> The ballroom on the floor above is said to be the largest in America. It is 18,000 square feet in area and large enough to accommodate 5000 persons. The floor is laid on floating cork and felt. There are no supporting pillars on either the

dance floor or theater auditorium, for the building is braced horizontally and vertically, involving new engineering principles. An indirect lighting system will be used.

Gabriel Beckman, mural artist, is in charge of decorating nine panels depicting a sequence of submarine scenes. Webber & Spaulding, Los Angeles architects, designed the building. Tom White, lessee, will operate the theater. He has charge of the opening, June 1.

In 1989, a cleaning and restoration of the Avalon theatre was made by Eva Matysek, whose philosophy was to disturb the sixty-year old art as little as possible. Thus, the house curtain was not touched at all.

The cleaning revealed many changes. For instance, the silver paint used behind many of the figures in the paintings had disappeared. Other background colors had also faded.

Over the six months period she worked on the murals, Matysek meticulously examined every inch, preparing precise colors and pigments, determining in most cases that when the backgrounds were repainted, the figures popped out in relief once more.

The result has been more than satisfactory. The theatre murals are now in excellent condition, as is the whole casino, thanks to the loving care of the then casino manager, Bill Delbart, who oversaw the whole project.

With the original opening of the casino and theatre on May 29, 1929, an occasion of celebration and festivity in Avalon complete with parade, the arrival of King Neptune, and hundreds of visitors, one might have assumed John Beckman's future as a muralist was assured. But in October of 1929, the stock market crashed, plunging the country into a depression, and forcing many to curtail cultural plans that now seemed superfluous.

Beckman was to have done the murals for the Los Angeles Country Club, but that project fell through, as did his proposed decorations for E. L. Doheny at the Petroleum building on Olympic Boulevard.

He did manage to complete murals for the Town House on Wilshire Boulevard, but work was hard to come by for a few years, and so John Beckman now turned to the motion picture studios where he knew his talents could be put to good use.

The studios in this period were involved in turning out entertainments to divert and amuse film patrons, helping them to forget the problems of the real world for a while. The studios appeared to be surviving handsomely in these economically perilous times.

Magic in the Movies

John Beckman began working in the film industry in 1934. He worked his way up through all the steps in the process to become finally an Art Director at Warner Brothers Studio. He worked on dozens of films at Warner Brothers and other studios while learning his craft. He well knew the importance of his work to a successful film. "Sets are like an actor," he said. "They are there all the time. They furnish a mood, a setting."

When one was employed by a studio art department in the 1930s-1940s, one typically began at the base of a pyramidal organization. Here were found the draftsmen who worked on blueprints, providing the details and dimensions of set pieces, like cornices, mouldings, and flats.

Sketch artists were also employed. These were skilled at making quick sketches, often in watercolor, valuable for showing the effect of light on objects. Then, above them, were the set designers, who worked out the look of the set, often providing palm trees, tables, chairs, rugs—whatever was needed for a particular scene.

Above them were the art directors, who provided the concepts and were known for their particular styles or expertise. These people had usually been in the business a long time and many of them worked consistently with certain directors who trusted their work and artistry. Usually, each studio had a head art director who oversaw the whole operation, especially the budget, and was a diplomatic person who could handle an out-of-control spendthrift with ease.

Warner Brothers' Studio in 1941, for instance, had the Head Art Director, and under him in the hierarchy, eight full-time Art Directors, plus a Chief

Draftsman who was accorded a lot of power and deference. Next came eleven Assistant Art Directors, followed by eighteen Set Designers, ten Sketch Artists, two Model Artists (who made maquettes, or models of the sets), and two Blue Print Operators, plus one secretary for the whole department, the only female employed in the whole department.

Today, the titles are even more elevated, with the head person often being designated as the Production Designer, and sometimes the set designers are referred to as Art Directors. With the advent of television, these terms spilled over into that medium, and, as films advanced in style from the beginning of the twentieth century, the special effects persons also gained more clout, with the result being that, today, they receive separate credits of their own and special recognition during awards ceremonies for films they work on, like *Star Wars* and *E.T.*

During the heyday of the studio system—1934-1952, highly respected art directors included Cedric Gibbons at M.G.M., Ross Bellah at Columbia, Anton Grot and John Beckman at Warner Brothers, and Hans Dreier at Paramount, among many others. They were responsible for everything seen behind the actor in a film.

The locations, moods, atmospheres they concocted set the tone for many of the movies audiences remember today—*The Gold Rush, Casablanca, Gone With the Wind, The Wizard of Oz, Gigi, Lawrence of Arabia, Jaws, Out of Africa, Dances with Wolves.* Consider how important the environment was in each of these films.

John Beckman best described the art director's job:

> The art director comes into the picture early. He, the writer, and the producer plan what to do. It takes time to build sets. Sometimes he can influence the director of the picture. He can sometimes save money by not going to Singapore or wherever.

Certain directors like to work with certain art directors. The art director is into the concept of the background, what it should look like.

The set designer drafts, makes drawings and sketches. He is concerned with the mechanics, the plans. You may have twenty, twenty-five set designers to help you. They make models, mock-ups, special effects.

Ross Bellah affords an entertaining picture of how one became an art director in the old days. He was hired at Columbia in 1934 as a temporary draftsman and remained for fifty-four years, becoming Columbia's head art director, working for the notorious Harry Cohn whom he saw on only two occasions:

Lionel Banks hired me for a couple of weeks, and I was only there for fifty-four years. I thought later that he said "I only need you for a couple of weeks" so that if I wasn't any good, he wouldn't be embarrassed to let me go. Well, I never ran out of work and I had things to do all the time, even though I'd never worked in a studio before.

I didn't know anything at all about sets, so at lunchtime when all the other draftsmen would go out to lunch, I'd go around to look at their drawings to see what they were doing and how they were doing it because I didn't know anything about what they did.

I'd only been in an architect's office working on real buildings, but sets are different. I didn't know how high they made the walls, for instance. So the first job that Lionel

Banks gave me, he made a little drawing, handed it to me, and said, "Here's the brownstone." I'd never even heard of a brownstone. I didn't know what it was. You know, I'm here in Hollywood working in an architect's office. I'm only in my twenties, so all I knew was Spanish architecture.

I didn't know New York and brownstone buildings. But I managed. Somehow I got by and stayed on. Later, they started calling the draftsmen set designers because it sounded more elegant. Art directors are now called Production Designers, you know. It's the same routine.

It was with an established art director that John Beckman's first two years—1934-1935—would be spent. His name was Richard Day (1896-1972), and he, significantly, had been the art director for most of director Erich von Stroheim's silent films at Universal, MGM, Paramount, and United Artists, including *Greed* and *Queen Kelly*.

A Canadian by birth, Day was renown for his intense realism in design. He won six Academy Awards for his work in films. His talents can be seen at their best in *Dodsworth* (1936), *Young Mr. Lincoln* (1939), *How Green Was My Valley* (1941), *A Streetcar Named Desire* (1951), and *On the Waterfront* (1954).

In 1934, John Beckman's apprenticeship with Richard Day began with *Nana*, an adaptation of Emil Zola's novel, starring Samuel Goldwyn's Garbo-like hope, Anna Sten, photographed by Gregg Toland, and directed by Dorothy Arzner. One could hardly have chosen a more prestigious production on which to begin one's career. The beautiful Russian actress, Anna Sten, made an impressive American debut as the tragic gamine in this film, even though her career never really caught on in the U.S.

Gregg Toland, famous later for his deep focus photography on *Wuthering Heights* (1939), *The Grapes of Wrath* (1940), and *Citizen Kane* (1941), had literally worked his way up from being an office boy to becoming Sam Goldwyn's chief cinematographer, and, perhaps the one more than any other who set the high standard for cinematography in films during the golden years.

The director of *Nana* was Dorothy Arzner (1900-1979), certainly a pioneer at this time. Her life story reads like a Hollywood script in itself. Her father owned a small restaurant in Hollywood in which Dorothy was a waitress and saw many movie people as customers. She went to the University of Southern California as a pre-med student, later worked on a newspaper, and drove an ambulance in World War I.

In movies, she began with William DeMille, who was brother to Cecil and father to Agnes, at Famous Players, working her way up from stenographer to script clerk, film cutter, and finally film editor.

Arzner was the editor on Rudolph Valentino's bullfighting scenes in *Blood and Sand* (1922). She then wrote film scripts, moving into direction in 1927 at Paramount, and continuing as a director until 1943. Among her directing assignments were *Christopher Strong* (1933) with Katharine Hepburn and *Craig's Wife* (1936) with Rosalind Russell.

During World War II, she produced training films for the W.A.C.s, then taught filmmaking at the Pasadena Playhouse and U.C.LA., finally making Pepsi Cola commercials for Joan Crawford. The kind of versatility and flexibility exemplified by Dorothy Arzner's career are not at all unusual in the lives of film directors.

In 1934, John Beckman also worked on *House of Rothschild* with Richard Day as art director, *Bulldog Drummond Strikes Back*, *The Affairs of Cellini*, and *Kid Millions*.

The common factor here is the enormous variety in settings he experienced, as well as styles. *The House of Rothschild*, with George Arliss, was a prestigious film about the famous banking family of Europe. It received an Academy Award nomination as Best Picture of 1934.

Bulldog Drummond Strikes Back was a top-notch Ronald Colman vehicle, a rousingly successful film in what passed for action-adventure in those days.

The Affairs of Cellini was a highbrow film about the Italian Renaissance goldsmith.

And *Kid Millions* was a slam-bang farcical musical in the Broadway manner starring Eddie Cantor and Ethel Merman.

One other unusual film Beckman worked on in his first year was *One Night of Love* which starred the glamorous opera singer, Grace Moore, and actor Tullio Carminati. The art director for this film was Stephen Goosson, who would later be the chief art director for Frank Capra films, including *Lost Horizon* (1937), on which John Beckman would do important work.

The following year, 1935, Beckman worked for Richard Day on four films, two of them directed by the brilliant Polish director, Richard Boleslavski—*Clive of India* and *Les Miserables*, a film version of the Victor Hugo novel.

Boleslavski had studied with and performed under Constantine Stanislavksy at the famed Moscow Art Theatre. He later would write a book on this method, *Six Lessons of Dramatic Art*, widely used by acting students. Among Boleslavski's films were *Rasputin and the Empress* (1933), starring John, Lionel and Ethel Barrymore, *The Painted Veil* (1934) with Greta Garbo, and *The Garden of Allah* with Marlene Dietrich and Charles Boyer (1936).

Working in these early years with both Richard Day and Richard Boleslavski, Beckman received significant training in the realistic and naturalistic film techniques, both of which forced set designers to be scrupulous in their research and accurate in every detail.

The film screen, magnifying the image twenty times larger than life, meant that everything had to be intensely realistic and truthful, because the entire mood or point of a scene could be ruined by one wrong, inaccurate detail.

Even the acting had to be unusually natural and understated. Observers said of Garbo that she never appeared to be acting at all. Yet when the rushes were viewed at the end of the day, they saw that her acting was of the subtlest, most believable style.

The other two Richard Day films in 1935 were the period piece *Cardinal Richelieu,* with George Arliss and Maureen O'Sullivan, and the glitzy musical *Folies Bergeres de Paris,* a Maurice Chevalier musical with Ann Sothern and Merle Oberon.

With this film, Beckman's apprenticeship period ended, as did his personal association with Richard Day. Beckman's son said that his father's only future reference to Richard Day was later in life when he said, "Oh, he's the head art director over at Fox."

The final 1935 motion picture Beckman worked on was a blockbuster—Shakespeare's *A Midsummer Night's Dream* co-directed by the great German directors, Max Reinhardt (1873-1943), and William Dieterle (1893-1972), with whom Beckman would work again on several quality films.

Reinhardt was a powerful force in the German theatre,well known for his huge extravaganzas and elaborate sets. Primarily a theatre director, Reinhardt, through this film production, helped popularize Shakespeare in America, offering a personable cast, including James Cagney as Bottom, Mickey Rooney as Puck, and Olivia de Havilland as Hermia.

It also introduced Anton Grot (1884-1974) as art director, a valued friend and colleague of John Beckman. The studio that produced *A Midsummer Night's Dream,* Warner Brothers, would become Beckman's and Grot's working home for many years after.

Anton Grot had been born in Poland. He studied design and illustration at the Kracow Art School and at the Technical High School in Konigsberg, Germany.

He began his film work in 1913, after having arrived in the United States in 1909. He did set designs for Lubin in Philadelphia, then worked in New York, finally landing in Hollywood where he worked for Cecil B. DeMille, Douglas Fairbanks and Mary Pickford at United Artists, and ultimately for Warner Brothers from 1927 to 1948.

He brought to all his work a European sense of expressionism, specializing in chiaroscuro effects of light and shadow on the screen. By so doing, he was able to convey a sense of mystery, a mood of forboding or doom, as in *Little Caesar* (1930) where his sets gave the unsavory impression of an evil underworld to reality, or in a Warners' musical, *Gold Diggers of 1933*, where his "Forgotten Man" set used huge angular shadows of downtrodden, defeated American veterans marching across a bridge.

Other films unmistakably designed by Grot were three Errol Flynn films, *Captain Blood* (1935), *The Private Lives of Elizabeth and Essex* (1939) and *The Sea Hawk* (1940), in all of which he created vivid environments, especially in the two dealing with the sea and sailing vessels which uncannily gave one the feeling of actually being there as an eye-witness. John Jr. remembers walking on board these sailing vessels with his father. He enjoyed it.

John Gabriel Beckman first met Anton Grot when Grot was working as associate designer on a Douglas Fairbanks' film, probably *The Thief of Bagdad* (1924). The two men would later work together on *Mildred Pierce* (1946) which won Joan Crawford an Academy Award.

In 1940, Grot received a special Academy Award for his invention of what was called a ripple machine. This device enabled designers to show light effects and different kinds of weather playing over ocean water.

Among the other films Grot worked on were *Robin Hood* (1922) and *The Thief of Bagdad* (1924), both for Douglas Fairbanks, *Dorothy Vernon of Haddon Hall* (1924) for Mary Pickford, *Outward Bound* (1930), *Mildred Pierce* (1946), and *The Two Mrs. Carrolls* (1947).

The sad ending of Anton Grot's career is that, as he grew older, the studio had less use for him. John Beckman, Jr., tells how Grot went east to visit relatives sometime in the 1940s, and, when he returned, he would show up at Warner Brothers, looking for work, but the studio kept putting him off, until finally he got the message and left.

John Jr. said he always assumed that his father would have to leave, also, when he reached sixty-five years of age. He never thought his father would stay in the business until his death at ninety-one.

Ironically, Anton Grot was the big man in the 1930s who helped the youthful Beckman in his career. As Beckman's star rose at Warner's, Grot's declined. In later years, Beckman tried to find work for his old friend, but to no avail. People never hear about these private backstage tragedies; they are not played out in public as are the lives of the star actors.

The co-director of *A Midsummer Night's Dream*, William Dieterle (1893-1972), was also an important professional colleague of John Beckman. Born in Ludwigshafen, Germany, he made his mark first as an actor in Germany and Switzerland, then he joined the Max Reinhardt troupe in Berlin in 1918. He soon began appearing in silent films, and finally directed his first film in 1924, *Der Mensch am Wege*, which featured a very young Marlene Dietrich beginning her career.

He concentrated on films from this point on, and was invited by Warner Brothers-First National to come to Hollywood in 1930. A large man who dramatically sported a big hat and white gloves on the set, one had no problem telling who was the director.

William Dieterle was also a man of refined taste and discrimination who numbered among his films *The Story of Louis Pasteur* (1936), *The Life of Emile Zola* (1937), *Juarez, The Hunchback of Notre Dame* (1939), and *Dr. Ehrlich's Magic Bullet* (1940), all distinguished by their seeming fidelity to actual events and naturalistic in their styles.

Not limited to one approach, however, Dieterle also directed two excellent romantic films starring Jennifer Jones, *Love Letters* (1945) and *Portrait of Jennie* (1949).

Although William Dieterle had become an American citizen in the late 1930s, his professional career and private life were severely damaged by the infamous Senator Joseph McCarthy and paranoid governmental authorities in the 1950s who disdained what they called his liberal films and twice engineered the confiscation of Dieterle's passport because of his sponsorship of Kurt Weill's and Bertolt Brecht's immigration to the United States. Work somehow became hard to find in a business and a country that were temporarily cowed by political bullies and cowards.

John Beckman's 1936-1937 films found him once again working for several different studios, notably Columbia and Twentieth-Century Fox, but also at

Warner Brothers, where he again worked with Anton Grot as art director and William Dieterle as director on *The Life of Emile Zola* starring Paul Muni.

Interesting that Beckman, who began his career working on the film version of Emile Zola's *Nana*, should now be engaged in a film biography of the great naturalistic novelist's life.

Other Warner Brothers' films he worked on included *The Petrified Forest*, the first of three Bette Davis films he would be associated with, and *The Prince and the Pauper*, his first Errol Flynn film and the first with art director, Robert Haas.

In 1936 he worked with William Darling, art director, on *Lloyds of London* for Twentieth-Century Fox and on *Mr. Deeds Goes to Town* with the Frank Capra-Stephen Goosson (art director)-Joseph Walker (cinematographer) team at Columbia.

Capra, like most directors, preferred to work with the same group of reliable people, and so in 1937 John Beckman again worked closely with this team on the highly acclaimed *Lost Horizon*, but more needs to be said about his important work on that film in a subsequent chapter.

With the sole exception of *The Rains Came* for Twentieth-Century Fox in 1939, all Beckman's work as set designer from 1937 to 1950 would be at Warner Brothers' Studio in Burbank.

Two of the films would again see him as part of the William Dieterle-Anton Grot team—on *Juarez* (1939) with Bette Davis, Paul Muni, and John Garfield and on *A Dispatch from Reuters* (1940) with Edward G. Robinson. Both these films had a quasi-documentary style about them and a European feeling, easily provided by Dieterle and Grot, and, one may imagine, by Beckman, who had his own European roots and experience.

In 1939 and 1941, Beckman did set design for two Humphrey Bogart films—*The Roaring Twenties* (1939) and *High Sierra* (1941), both directed by Raoul Walsh (1887-1980), known for his tough-guy action films in a no-holds-barred realistic style. These two films also set the mold for Humphrey Bogart's definitive film style and for the kind of hard-edged product many people associated with Warner Brothers.

Raoul Walsh is another colorful film director whose career lasted many years and whose life-story reads like one of his own movies. He is most closely identified with his well-controlled action films, although he did direct some odd films like *Going Hollywood* (1933), *The Strawberry Blonde*, a Rita Hayworth-James Cagney-Olivia de Havilland musical delight (1941), and *The Horn Blows at Midnight* (1944) with Jack Benny, thus providing the comedian with one of his longest running gags.

A native New Yorker, Raoul Walsh had an extraordinary upbringing, sailing to Cuba in 1903 with his uncle who was captain of a ship, learning to ride and rope in Mexico, working at odd jobs as a wrangler, undertaker, doctor's assistant before becoming an actor, playing roles as cowboys in silent films, assisting D. W. Griffith at Biograph, following him to Hollywood, appearing as John Wilkes Booth in Griffith's *The Birth of a Nation* (1915), making a documentary about the life of Pancho Villa in Mexico, and later working with such silent film stars as Valentino, Theda Bara, and Douglas Fairbanks.

In 1928, he lost an eye when a jackrabbit crashed through the windshield of his car, and forever after he became identified as the director with the eye patch, a look that gave him deserved extra respect from casts and crews.

He also had the distinction of introducing John Wayne in films in *The Big Trail* (1930) and becoming known as a man's director, working later with Clark Gable, James Cagney, and, of course, Bogart.

Walsh's best-known films include *What Price Glory?* (1926), *They Died With Their Boots On* (1941), *White Heat* (1949), as well as the two Bogart films. In 1955, he directed *Battle Cry* and hired John Beckman to be the art director for this action film starring Van Heflin, Aldo Ray, and Dorothy Malone.

Two Humphrey Bogart classics for which Beckman did set design were *The Maltese Falcon* (1941) and *Casablanca* (1942). *The Maltese Falcon* marked John Huston's first directorial effort. He also wrote the screenplay for it, adapted from Dashiell Hammett's novel. Humphrey Bogart played detective Sam Spade in a cast that included Mary Astor, Sydney Greenstreet, and Peter Lorre. The film has been widely praised for the taut, suspenseful detective melodrama it is. The sets, props (art direction by Robert Haas), and cinematography by Arthur Edeson all worked beautifully in this compelling film.

Of special interest on this film was a young actress named Arlene Russell. Born Velma Lois Elaine Zachery, she was appearing in *The Maltese Falcon* as Arlene Russell, but would later legally change her name to Layne Grey. She would become John Gabriel Beckman's second wife years later.

Beckman also began a lasting friendship with Mary Astor on this film. Jane Beckman, daughter of Layne Grey and John Gabriel Beckman, remembers: "I recall his visiting her (Mary Astor) regularly while I was growing up."

For *Casablanca*, Beckman worked with Carl Jules Weyl, a talented art director, who became ill during the making of this film so that Beckman had to finish it for him. Weyl later died of leukemia at the young age of thirty-nine.

The final scene in *Casablanca*, at the airport in the fog where Bogart (as Rick) says goodbye to Ingrid Bergman (as Ilsa) is what Beckman contributed.

It was economically filmed at the Warner Brothers' Studio in Burbank, although, through the special magic of the screen and the artistry of the designers and technicians, it creates all the mystery and intrigue of a foggy airport in Casablanca.

Directed by Michael Curtiz, whom Beckman would work with many more times in the future, the film won Academy Awards in 1943 for Best Picture, Best Director, and Best Screenplay. The cinematographer again was Arthur Edeson.

The film is perhaps the apogee of the Warner Brothers' distinctive style—a black and white, realistic treatment of a recognizable social or political problem in a believable, no-frills setting, this time with a romantic entanglement and an unsentimental conclusion.

Following *The Maltese Falcon*, John Huston directed *Across the Pacific* (1942) for Warners, again using Robert Haas as art director, along with Hugh Reticker, and Arthur Edeson as cinematographer.

Humphrey Bogart and Mary Astor were the stars of this World War II film, which attempted to capture the spirit and flavor of the war in the Pacific. John Beckman was a set designer for this film as well as for Michael Curtiz' version of the Irving Berlin musical *This Is The Army* (1942), which featured a future president, Ronald Reagan, in the cast.

When he worked with Arthur Edeson and John Huston on *The Maltese Falcon* and *Across the Pacific*, Beckman was working with two of the best in the business.

Arthur Edeson (1891-1970), a graduate of City University of New York, began as a portrait photographer, entered silent films in 1911, and soon worked with Douglas Fairbanks, first as a cameraman and then as director of photography on such films as *Robin Hood* (1922) and *The Thief of Bagdad* (1924).

When sound came in, Edeson was cinematographer for *All Quiet on the Western Front* (1930), *Frankenstein* (1931), *Mutiny on the Bounty* (1935).

Skilled at black and white photography, at Warner Brothers Edeson filmed *They Drive By Night* (1940), *The Maltese Falcon* (1941), *The Male Animal*, *Casablanca*, and *Across the Pacific* (all 1942).

One of the founders of the American Society of Cinematographers, Arthur Edeson retired from the industry in 1949.

John Huston (1906-1987), on the other hand, led a legendary, picaresque life, rivaling that of his literary contemporary, Ernest Hemingway. Married and divorced five times, Huston was the son of actor Walter Huston and father of film actress Anjelica Huston.

His colorful life included stints as a street musician in London, artist in Paris, officer in the Mexican cavalry, prize fighter, lord of the manor in Ireland, as well as screenwriter, actor, and director in Hollywood. Strongly interested in art and its relationship to film, his film *Moulin Rouge* (1952) pays homage to that interest and to Huston's own idol, Henri Toulouse-Lautrec.

His best films often deal with characters caught in survival situations, like *The Treasure of Sierra Madre* and *Key Largo* (both 1948), *The Asphalt Jungle* (1950),

The African Queen and *Red Badge of Courage* (both 1951), and *Moby Dick* (1956).

As writer and director, Huston always probed serious themes in his films. His last films were *Prizzi's Honor* (1985), which won daughter Anjelica an Academy Award, and *The Dead* (1987), adapted from James Joyce's short story. Few directors can boast such an enviable track record.

For the rest of the 1940s, Beckman worked as set decorator primarily with Anton Grot and Robert Haas on a series of commendable films. With Grot, he did *Mildred Pierce* (1945), a black-hearted film that won Joan Crawford an Oscar, *Rhapsody in Blue* (1945), a film biography of composer George Gershwin, and *The Two Mrs. Carrolls* (1947), a talky, lurid melodrama starring Humphrey Bogart, Barbara Stanwyck, and Alexis Smith, in which Bogart played an artist who murders his wife for a new love interest.

Toward the close of Grot's career at Warner Brothers, Beckman worked with him on a Doris Day vehicle, *Romance on the High Seas* (1948), directed by Michael Curtiz. Grot would have only two more films, a Bette Davis comedy, *June Bride* (1948) and a film prophetically called *Backfire* (1950) before his work would terminate for Warner Brothers and he would be put out to pasture to paint. Beckman's career, on the contrary, was on the rise.

With Robert Haas (1887-1962) as art director, Beckman worked on *Mr. Skeffington* (1944) with Bette Davis and Claude Rains, *Johnny Belinda* (1948), a film about a deaf-mute played by Jane Wyman, who won an Academy Award for her role in this moody, atmospheric film, and *The Glass Menagerie* (1950), the first film version of Tennesse Williams' stage play with Gertrude Lawrence, Kirk Douglas, and Jane Wyman.

Haas' work on these films was of a high order. He was one of Warner Brothers' most reliable art directors during the 1930s and 1940s. Born in New Jersey in 1887, he had been educated at the University of Pennsylvania and had begun in films in 1920 when he worked with Jesse Lasky.

He was a favorite art director for Bette Davis, working with her on *Jezebel* (1938), *Dark Victory* and *The Old Maid* (both 1939), *The Man Who Came To*

Dinner (1941), *Mr. Skeffington* (1944), *A Stolen Life* (1946), and *Beyond the Forest* (1949), the film in which she uttered the famous words, "What a dump!" Haas provided the dump that she and her husband, Joseph Cotton, playing a doctor, lived in near the railroad tracks in dreary Moline, Illinois.

One last film worthy of mention in Beckman's set design period is *Arsenic and Old Lace* (1944), a film that perennially shows up on late-night television. Directed by Frank Capra and starring Cary Grant in an uncharacteristic role, the film also boasts the magnificent Josephine Hull, repeating her stage performance, plus Peter Lorre, Edward Everett Horton, and Jack Carson doing comic turns.

The set is primarily the interior of two eccentric sisters' home in Brooklyn, filled with all the appropriate left-over Victorian bric-a-brac, anti-macassars, and coffin-life furniture one might associate with people of that period.

The film is a quirky comedy, the sort of stage play the Warner Brothers liked to try every so often. As with their versions of *The Man Who Came to Dinner* and *The Voice of the Turtle*, both successful Broadway stage comedies, the results were, at best, a little heavy-handed. Laughs were not really Warner Brothers' strong suit.

Another professional experience during this period was the Strike of 1937, which affected Beckman as it did other members in the industry.

Out of the strike came the Society of Motion Picture Art Directors. The set designers already had their own union. In the early 1930s, the studios would hire a crew, keep them on for a picture of two, lay them off, hire another crew for less money, keep them on, then lay them off too, and hire the first crew back at even less money. This prompted the strike.

Later, in the early 1950s, the set designers joined I.A.T.S.E.—the International Alliance of Theatrical Stage Employees, which is affiliated with the AFL-CIO.

The unusual opportunity that John Beckman had, working with some of the most imaginative directors, artists, photographers, costumers, lighting designers, writers, and actors was invaluable. And he, with his own skills as an artist and a man with vision, plus his incredible quiet determination and ability to stay calm in the middle of creative crises, moved him right along to become one of the most valued, reliable persons in the business.

Was it any wonder, then, that in 1937, when Frank Capra's art director, Stephen Goosson, was looking for someone skilled in Oriental design to design the lamasery for *Lost Horizon*, a set decorator said to him, "Why don't you get John Beckman? He's the best there is."

Goosson had previously worked with Beckman on *One Night of Love* (1934) and *Mr. Deeds Goes To Town* (1936), and he certainly had noticed his exquisite murals in Grauman's Chinese Theatre. So John was brought in as a designer for this motion picture to be directed by the hot new director, Frank Capra.

Being there with the talent at the right time and place: That's so often the name of the game in theatre and film.

Lost Credit for Lost Horizon

No American director in the 1930s garnered more praise and awards for his work than Frank Capra (1897-1991). After his clean sweep of the Academy Awards in 1934 with the light-hearted comedy *It Happened One Night* the film world was his. He followed it up with a string of hits—*Mr. Deeds Goes to Town, Lost Horizon, You Can't Take It With You,* and *Mr. Smith Goes to Washington.*

Again, typical of Hollywood film directors, his own life was perhaps his best picture. He had been born in Palermo, Sicily, emigrated to the United States with his family when he was six, lived in southern California where he worked his way through Cal Tech, graduated as a chemical engineer, enlisted in the army as a private, rose to becoming a second lieutenant, drifted for a while, and then directed his first film with absolutely no idea of what he was doing, received $75 for it, liked it, and worked his way up, until he became a gag writer for Hal Roach, and then wrote and directed the comedian, Harry Langdon's films until the jealous Langdon fired him, prompting Capra to leave for New York where he directed a film that flopped, sending him back to Hollywood where he worked for Mack Sennett, until he signed a contract to direct for Harry Cohn at Columbia Pictures on Poverty Row. This deal couldn't have been better—for Capra or Columbia. Together, they made history.

Since Columbia was considered the bottom in a Hollywood where MGM and Paramount were the top, the feisty, but sensible Cohn, gave Capra a free rein to do what he wanted. At first, Capra's films were fairly routine, but on a Jean Harlow film *Platinum Blonde* (1931), he met Robert Riskin, a screenwriter, who spoke his language, resulting in a partnership that worked perfectly through Capra's greatest successes in the 1930s.

Another aspect of Capra's work was his knack of working with actors and actresses who had unusual voices. He directed Barbara Stanwyck in *Ladies of Leisure* (1930) and was responsive to the power of that actress' throaty voice as an instrument of persuasion. He later directed her in *The Bitter Tea of General Yen* (1933) and *Meet John Doe* (1941) where, as a reporter, she actually fed words to an inarticulate Gary Cooper, playing John Doe, to read to the public gathered in a ballpark.

Another actress whose vocal qualities appealed to Capra (and to audiences) was Jean Arthur, whose cheerful chipmunk voice graced his *Mr. Deeds Goes to Town* (1936), *You Can't Take It With You* (1938), and *Mr. Smith Goes to Washington* (1939).

For some of his actors he provided telling-off speeches like the one in *Mr. Smith Goes to Washington* where the idealistic Jimmy Stewart, in his distinctive halting, sensitive voice, uses a filibuster to tell off congressional bureaucrats, or in his later *It's a Wonderful Life* (1946) where Stewart again (as George Bailey) shouts his affirmation of life through the town of Bedford Falls when he realizes that he wants to live instead of committing suicide.

Searching for an actor to play the high-minded Robert Conway in *Lost Horizon*, Capra looked no farther than Ronald Colman, whose velvety baritone voice had already thrilled audiences when, as Sydney Carton, he uttered those memorable lines at the conclusion of *A Tale of Two Cities* (1935—directed by Jack Conway for David Selznick at MGM): "It's a far, far better thing that I do, than I have ever done; it's a far, far better rest that I go to, than I have ever known."

Capra also appreciated the theatrical taciturnity of Gary Cooper, the clean-cut All-American man of few words, using this quality to play off against the husky-voiced, loquacious Barbara Stanwyck in *Meet John Doe* (1941), not just in the ballpark scene but throughout the film.

What Capra and Riskin's characters were giving voice to were probably the two men's own views about what constituted solid American virtues—honesty, courage, a kind of fundamental optimism and belief that things could be changed for the better. This caused some critics and audiences to turn away from Capra's films as being too simplistic for our complex times. One should remember that *It's a Wonderful Life* was not particularly well-received when it first opened in 1946, but now is widely shown on television every Christmas with the special blessing of Jimmy Stewart who always touted it as his favorite film.

Capra's main influence in film was definitely in the 1930s. He directed two of the finest screwball comedies of the period—*It Happened One Night* (1934*)* and *You Can't Take It With You* (1938), and he was instrumental in promoting two of his daffy heroines, Jean Arthur and Claudette Colbert as comic geniuses, and one, Barbara Stanwyck, as a formidable balanced woman of earthy intelligence.

During World War II, Frank Capra returned to the U.S. Army, now as a major, and made propaganda films for the United States, but when the war was over, he met with indifferent success in movies, probably because his easy optimism was out of sync with that period of adjustment. His best work in this period was the film version of *Arsenic and Old Lace* (1945) featuring the distinctive voices and personalities of Cary Grant and Josephine Hull and *It's a Wonderful Life*, the Jimmy Stewart classic.

He directed a so-so Katharine Hepburn-Spencer Tracy comedy about Washington politics, *State of the Union* (1948) and a Bette Davis-Glenn Ford film, *A Pocketful of Miracles* (1961), but the old magic didn't work so well this time, and the Capra career went into an eclipse. Signficantly, his excellent autobiography is entitled *Frank Capra: The Name Above the Title* (1971). He earned it, every inch of the way.

In 1934, however, when *It Happened One Night* captured all the major Academy Awards, the first film to make such a clean sweep, Frank Capra was the salvation of Columbia Pictures, moving that studio and its boss, the tempestuous Harry Cohn, into the front ranks. This was the year Ross Bellah reported for work under Lionel Banks in the Art Department and the year John Beckman began his work for Samuel Goldwyn on the set of *Nana*.

In 1936, Capra had another success in *Mr. Deeds Goes to Town* with Gary Cooper playing the rich, eccentric, tuba-playing Deeds who is bent on giving away twenty million dollars he's inherited. Of course, he's abetted by the charming, squeaky-voiced Jean Arthur in a cast that included gravel-voiced Lionel Stander and True Brit Raymond Walburn, among others. Capra picked up another Oscar as best director for this one.

John Beckman worked on this film at Columbia under the aegis of Capra's art director, Steve Goosson, and found himself working with another talented man in the art department, Ross Bellah.

In that year also, Frank Capra began production on his film version of James Hilton's novel *Lost Horizon*. His art director was Steve Goosson, who realized he needed someone capable of designing an oriental set for Shangri-La. Ross Bellah explains what happened next:

> John was pretty well-known already around Hollywood and Los Angeles because he did Grauman's Chinese and Catalina and all those things. And I remember one of the set designers that was there, telling the boss, Steve Goosson, "'You know, you ought to get John Beckman. He's the best there is." I heard him tell him that, you know, because I was there. This was for *Lost Horizon*.
>
> And Steve brought John in and John designed *Lost Horizon*. He first designed it as more factual background, and then, through the process, they eliminated it; they wanted to make it more unrealistic and modern, and he did, and made it terrific. As a matter of fact, John didn't get the Oscar, but Steve did. Steve went up and got the Oscar (for best interior set decoration), but I know because I was there, and I saw who actually did the designs.

Bellah maintains that Beckman designed all the sets for the picture. He explains that Goosson was the head art director, but, typically, delegated the actual work to others in the department.

After the success of the film, and over the passage of time, others have claimed they designed the sets, but Bellah disputes this. He is firm in his belief that John Beckman designed the sets, even though he received no screen credit. Only Steve Goosson was credited.

"I know John was the designer because I was in the room with him," Bellah states. " I did some of the detailing. He was designing it, and if there was something that needed to have a larger-scale drawing made of it, I would do it, under his direction, of course. This seems strange, because, years later in television, he would work for me for years. So John designed the whole thing. Of course, he couldn't do all the details. He wouldn't have had the time. There's a time frame for these things to get done. Not only I, but some of the other fellows did other details. It was an exciting time." Bellah adds, "Nobody could draw like John. He was simply a genius."

The reason credit for designing this movie becomes important is that the literary concept of Shangri-La was visualized for millions of people through the imaginative sets. Naturally, the whole project was a collaborative effort, as is everything in the theatre or film.

It is entirely understandable that everyone who works on a project like this wants to receive recognition for his or her share of the work. Someone has to discuss the initial concept with the producer and director. That would have been the head art director—Steve Goosson— and then, he, in turn, has to discuss it with his art directors and set designers, who, in turn, discuss it with their technicians, until the whole is realized, when only Steve Goosson's name will appear in the credits on the screen.

Bellah's view is that Goosson leaned heavily on Beckman, entrusting him with the design sketches and the revisions, until the concept was realized to Frank Capra's satisfaction.

Capra, himself, did a lot of research on Tibet, where most of the film takes place. He hired explorer-photographer, Harrison Forman, who had photographed Tibet, to be technical advisor, and immersed himself in studying both the geography and anthropology of that small country.

The story on which the film is based is one of three novels by English writer James Hilton that were made into extremely successful films. The others were *Goodbye Mr. Chips* (1939) with Robert Donat and Greer Garson and *Random Harvest* (1942) with Garson and Ronald Colman, both made at MGM.

The way Frank Capra came across *Lost Horizon* is one of those happy Hollywood flukes. On his way up to a USC-Stanford game in Palo Alto with his crusty boss, Harry Cohn, Capra noticed the title *Lost Horizon* on a newsstand in Los Angeles' Union Station. He remembered that Alec Woolcott had praised this book in his regular radio broadcast, and so Capra bought it to read on the train.

The story impressed him—an idealistic foreign secretary from England, kidnapped and brought to Shangri-La where he meets the High Lama, who lives in a perfect society, free from war, poverty, and problems of all kinds—and, further, the High Lama decides that Robert Conway, the foreign secretary, is the right man to be his successor.

A dream man in a dream world—just right for Capra, who, somewhere along the line, decided that he wanted to do only films with important messages—usually the honest individual struggling against the crooks of the world.

In the dining car the next morning, Capra told Cohn he wanted to do the film, that only Ronald Colman could play the leading part, and that the film would cost two million dollars. Cohn was smart. Without bothering to read the book, he agreed, because he knew he had a hot filmmaker with talent and style opposite him.

The fantastic sets for Shangri-La were built on the Columbia Ranch on Hollywood Way in Burbank. Ross Bellah talks about the Ranch then and now:

They built the whole exterior there. Do you know that thing was there through the years, and it got remodeled into other things. The Japanese bought Columbia, but they sold the ranch to Warner Brothers who own the ranch now.

We used to have, across the street from the Columbia Ranch, forty acres of open field. A lot of westerns were done out there on the forty acres. You were out in the open.

This went on for years until—and this broke our hearts—they sold the forty acres. I think they sold it for a million dollars.

Now there are condominiums and all all over town. There's a market, a whole shopping center.

John Beckman, Jr., too, recalls watching the Shangri-La set being built when he was a boy. His father always maintained that he was proudest of his work on *Lost Horizon* of all the sets he worked on for the studios.

For Capra, finding actors to portray Tibetans was a problem. Tibetans, he felt, were taller than the Chinese or Japanese. He used Pala Indians from the San Diego area who were very convincing in their roles, and, for the ancient High Lama, he got an incredible performance from Sam Jaffe, who was only thirty-eight years old at the time. Paired opposite the impeccable British actor, Ronald Colman, the transfer of power from the High Lama to Robert Conway made perfect sense.

Oddly enough, the film was a complete disaster at its Santa Barbara sneak preview. The audience, hoping to see the MGM Lion with the lofty *Ars gratia artis* pronouncement beneath it, or the snow-covered Paramount mountain, instead saw Columbia's Torch Lady logo and broke into loud groans of disapproval. Then they began to laugh ten minutes into the film, ruining the entire mood Capra was aiming for.

Capra himself ran into a man at the water fountain in the lobby who, not knowing who he was, said, "Did you ever see such a Goddamned Fu Manchu thing in your life? People who made it should be shot."

Capra decided to burn the first two reels and start the film with the burning of Baskul and the airplane pulling away from the field. This made all the difference, and the film now connected correctly with its audiences. Obviously, it takes not only vision and talent, but also daring and a strong stomach to whip a film into its proper shape.

The version of *Lost Horizon* that we see today includes one hundred thirty-two minutes of soundtrack, but only one hundred twenty-five minutes of black and white picture. From the moment of its release in 1937, several shortened versions of the film were shown throughout the world.

In 1967, it was discovered that the original nitrate film was pretty much gone, so the version that has survived is missing twenty-five minutes. The current video version fills in the missing time with freeze-framed shots or photo stills from the original production while we listen to the soundtrack flow continuously.

In 1973, a restoration of *Lost Horizon* was begun, under the direction of Robert Gitt, by the National Center for Film and Video Preservation, along with the British Film Institute, Columbia Classics, the Motion Picture Broadcasting and Recorded Sound Division of the Library of Congress, and the U.C.L.A. Film, Television, and Radio Archives. Frank Capra, himself, also worked on the restoration, drawing on material housed in the Frank Capra Archives at Wesleyan University in Middletown, Connecticut.

At the 1937 Academy Awards, *Lost Horizon* won for Best Interior Decoration (Stephen Goosson) and Best Editing (Gene Havlick and Gene Milford). It also received nominations for Best Picture, Best Supporting Actor (H. B. Warner), Best Sound, Best Score (Dimitri Tiomkin), and Best Assistant Director (C.C. Coleman, Jr.).

The original credits on the film read:

Photographer   Joseph Walker

Aerial Photographer   Elmer Dyer

Technical Advisor   Harrison Forman

Screenplay   Robert Riskin
   (from the novel by James Hilton)

Film Editors   Gene Havlick
                Gene Milford

Special camera effects
                E. Roy Davidson
                Ganahl Carson

Art Director   Stephen Goosson

Costumer   Ernst Dryden

Musical Score   Dimitri Tiomkin

Musical Director   Max Steiner

CAST

Robert Conway   Ronald Colman

Sondra   Jane Wyatt

Lovett   Edward Everett Horton

George Conway   John Howard

Barnard   Thomas Mitchell

Maria   Margo

Gloria   Isabel Jewell

Chang   H. B. Warner

High Lama   Sam Jaffe

    The Hall Johnson Choir was used to provide background singing, chanting, and humming.

    What one sees and hears as the picture plays is the result of the director's collaboration with the scenic artists, sound people, costumers, make-up people, technicians, writers, photographers, and actors. Consider *Lost Horizon* now through the eyes of a prospective art director:

    As the beginning credits roll, we see images of snow-covered Himalayan mountains with ominous dark clouds floating by intermingled with fluffy white ones. Then, the screen becomes a scroll unfolding, while the following words from the novel roll:

In these days of wars and rumors of wars—haven't you ever dreamed of a place where there was peace and security, where living was not a struggle but a lasting delight?

Of course you have.

So has every man since Time began. Always the same dream. Sometimes he calls it Utopia—Sometimes the Fountain of Youth—Sometimes merely 'that little chicken farm.'

One man had such a dream and saw it come true.

He was Robert Conway—England's 'Man of the East'—soldier, diplomat, public hero—

Our story starts in the war-torn Chinese city of Baskul, where Robert

Conway has been sent
to evacuate ninety white
people before they are
butchered in a local
revolution.

Baskul—
the night of March 10,
1935.

In black and white, we see a scene of great
urgency. People are running toward planes at night in
an airport. Robert Conway, carrying a small boy,
pushes through the middle of the crowd. Conway lets
the boy off, pushes through to a telephone, shouts
into it that he needs more planes.

We see people setting gas drums on fire at the
airport to burn the hangers. The hangers are being
burned to light the way for the airplanes because the
electricity has gone off. Vivid images of planes and
flames. We see Robert Conway get on an airplane with
other cast members, just as the crowd attacks.

At the pilot's door, something odd happens. It
looks as though there was a last-minute change of
pilot, then the plane takes off.

The next scene is the interior of the airplane. We
see the cast talking, revealing themselves to one
another. Lovett is a paleontologist, hunting fossils. He
has unearthed the vertebrae of an animal found only
in Asia. He is proud of this discovery, expecting it will
establish him in science and make him famous. He
tells this to Barnard, who is wearing a golf hat, and
who appears to be hearty, but somewhat cynical.

Gloria, an overly-made-up blonde from Chicago,
talks tough and coughs a lot, as though she is dying
of tuberculosis.

Robert and George Conway, brothers, sit next to
each other, drinking and getting drunker, as though
weary, exhausted, after the conflict and flight.

George appears to be younger, more nervous. He
keeps talking about how Robert will probably become
the next Foreign Secretary for England.

Robert is an Anthony Eden type of man,
dashing, well-spoken, calm in crisis, a natural leader.

But, as he drinks, Robert wryly says to his brother: "Did you say (in your cable) we saved ninety white people? Hooray. Did you say we left ten thousand natives behind down there to be annihilated?"

As the plane travels through the air, Barnard comments to Lovett, "We're supposd to be traveling east, aren't we? It looks to me as though we're traveling west."

The passengers now discover they have been shanghaied. An Oriental pilot has been substituted for the British one. The Chinese pilot opens the door into the passenger area and brandishes a gun at the passengers. Gloria screams hysterically. The others are alarmed, all, of course, except Robert Conway who says he's going to take a nap and will worry about it when they land.

The next scene shows a landing of the plane somewhere in what appears to be Mongolia. Villages. Sheep. Bayonets. Refueling. The sound track switches to clanging Mongolian-like cymbals and music.

Suddenly, the screen shoots news reports at us from around the world. A headline in a Shanghai paper reads, "CONWAY IS MISSING." We go to No. 10 Downing Street in London, where a meeting of officials has hastily been called.

Back to the plane again, in cold, snowy country now, over high mountain peaks. We see the plane's altimeter reading, first, 18,000 feet, and, then, 24,000 feet. Gloria is hysterical again and screams because she can't breathe. The pilot opens the door from the cockpit and throws in an oxygen tank to her. Conway and Company administer it to her.

Abruptly, the plane's engine sputters. The plane is faltering, flopping through the sky. We see the Himalayas at a crazy angle now. Snow. Ice. The plane skids in for a dangerous landing with the passengers huddled in the rear of the plane in a futile attempt to balance it. The passengers exit into the windy snowscape.

Robert discovers that the pilot died at the controls. He finds a map on his body. "We're in unexplored country," says Robert. Robert and George go out to search for food. They bring back mountain grass into the plane for the passengers to eat.

From the window of the plane, we see porters approaching through the snow, a long fur-clad line of them. The passengers go out to meet them. A gentle, well-spoken man says, "I am from the nearby lamasery. My name is Chang."

The passengers, now outfitted by the porters with heavy fur coats, boots and hoods, begin a strenuous journey through the snow. They use ropes for climbing. There is much pulling. Up mountains. Over rope bridges. Bridging crevasses and negotiating tricky mountain peaks.

Suddenly, we get our first view of the Valley of the Blue Moon and Shangri-La. It is futuristic, ultra-modern, closely resembling Le Corbusier's city of Chandigarh in the Punjab, India. There is a tall, pavilion-like whiteness and purity about the place. It gives the appearance of being an architect's dream village—a generous helping of tall columns, orchards, fountains, an absence of wind and treachery—the opposite from the wintry landscape Conway and company have been traveling through.

The next scene moves into the interior of the lamasery. We are in a dining room. The ceilings are very high. There are tall columns, torchere lamps. The interior looks like Frank Lloyd Wright's Hollyhock House in Hollywood. There is a massive table, consoles, sconces with candles in them on the walls.

The camera now cuts to the Valley of the Blue Moon and pans it so that we fully appreciate everything we're seeing. There are circles and semi-circles in the architectural design. Windows sometimes have octagonal patterns, diamonds, rectangles, odd geometric designs. There are *jets d'eaux* in the gardens. The look is similar to that which will appear in the New York World's Fair of 1939—futuristic, modern, as it was called then. There are graceful inclined walks up to the buildings. There are pergolas.

We see a wholesome-looking woman, Sondra, on a white horse. A waterfall. Then Sondra swimming nude, chaste, innocent. Violin music on the sound track. Robert Conway comes by and inadvertently happens upon this scene. Sondra notices that he has observed her. The scene is one of harmless eroticism.

In the next scene, we see Barnard confessing that he was really a scoundrel named Chalmers Bryant and swindled people. He began as a plumber. Built up his business. Then the stock market crashed. After that, he was regarded as a crook.

Suddenly, George Conway, always on edge, goes berserk, and fires a gun. Chang, explaining Shangri-La's concept to the hostages, is soft-spoken, reasonable, with a pleasant, educated English accent.

The doorways in the interior scenes are sometimes hexagonal. Robert Conway passes through one on his way to visit the High Lama. He notices that the High Lama is really Father Perrault (the founder of Shangri-La). He has only one leg and must be two hundred years old at least. The High Lama says, "There are moments in every man's life when he glimpses the eternal." The High Lama said he read this in one of Robert Conway's own books.

Conway listens carefully to everything this mysterious man says and is obviously impressed by the High Lama and his philosophy.

While we overhear, we also notice that there is a lot of interesting grillwork in some doorways of the set.

We cut now to scenes of sheep and shepherds. We see Robert Conway among artisans and the ordinary people of Shangri-La. Now he is among schoolchildren. He dismisses them gently. Pigeons fly through the air. We see Sondra, the teacher. We hear flute music We are now in a Robert Conway-Sondra romantic scene, very pretty, idyllic, and chaste.

Next, through a striking peacock-grill door, we see Maria and George Conway, who are beginning a romantic encounter of their own.

Then we hear chimes ringing on a church-like structure with a stylized celtic cross thrust into the frame.

The camera cuts back to Sondra and Robert walking through a bower where wistaria vines curl in an arranged manner around columns. There is a light humor in this romantic scene. They kiss. In the background, one sees a version of the classic Hermes as fleet-footed messenger statue.

Back to other characters on whom Shangri-La's special magic is working: Barnard wants to put a reservoir and a whole plumbing system in the valley; Lovett wants to teach children in the village; Gloria now has removed her garish make-up and seems more tranquil. Only George remains unchanged, still nervous and unpredictable.

The camera next cuts to a chess match between Chang and Robert Conway in the dining room set. Chang says, "Age is a limit we impose upon ourselves." We see Barnard showing Gloria his plumbing plans.

Now George appears. He wants to leave. He has the porters coming. But Lovett says he has started his classes and refuses to leave. The others state they will not leave either, only George.

A torchlight parade of people crosses Shangri-La. We see staircases. Many columns. A polished floor. Grillwork on doors. A lagoon in front of a building that looks remarkably like the Russian pavilion at the 1939 World's Fair in New York, a building with a central entrance flanked by two massive rectangular wings and stairs going up in the middle.

A long, mystical scene with the High Lama and Robert Conway, in which the High Lama passes on his high mission to Robert. The High Lama's last words: "I place in your hands, my son, the future and destiny of Shangri-La."

Robert now tells George what has transpired. George doesn't believe it, thinks it's a sham, a fraud. In this scene, there are two oil portraits of women on the walls, reminiscent of Reynolds or Rembrandt.

Sometimes the chairs have a quasi-Chinese Chippendale look. The candlestick holder with a scroll in it looks like Spanish iron work, something you might find in William Randolph Hearst's San Simeon. The interiors, in fact, often look like restrained San Simeon.

Maria is now seen, saying she wants to leave Shangri-La with George. She tells him she has only been there two and a half years, not as long as Chang said she has been there. Maria is lying. George and Maria convince Robert that he should leave also, that he has been deceived. Convinced, Robert decides to go with them.

The camera cuts to a path by mountainous caves. The Conway brothers, Maria, and porters are crossing a bridge that leads out of the valley. We see Sondra running after Robert, but she stops and does not go beyond a certain point.

Wind swirls up on the screen. There is a long shot of Robert and the porters in the Himalayan mountain snow. We hear echoes on the sound track. We see the porters traversing slippery glaciers. Now, the porters are firing guns, a dangerous symbol of the outside world. Their firing triggers an avalanche of snow.

We see both Conways and Maria in severe snow and wind squalls. Maria falls. Maria withers up. She becomes an aged, wrinkled crone before our eyes.

The Conways take shelter in a cave. There are huge stalactites. They lay Maria down. She is ancient, hundreds of years old. George suffers revulsion at the sight and half jumps, half falls to a bruising death in the mountains.

The camera zooms in on Robert, who is lost in thought. Snow. Wind. Fur Parka. Sky, rocks, snow, wind—all the elements of the earth are shown. The choir is chanting. We see Robert with a shepherd's crook walking back toward Shangri-La. He falters, falls. The sun comes out. Robert walks in silhouette on the mountain. We see the snow tumbling down over a cave. Stalactites of snow. Robert staggers again and falls. Some villagers find him.

The screen flashes newspaper headlines:

"CONWAY FOUND ALIVE IN CHINESE MISSION"

Cut to No. 10 Downing Street. Government officials are buzzing about how Conway has suffered a loss of memory. Correspondent Gainsford in Manchuria says Conway wants to return to Tibet, is determined to get back to some mysterious place there.

Cut to London in fog. The St. George Club. Men are talking. Drinks. Gainsford among them, explaining that Conway is a puzzle to him. He relates that Conway had many adventures, strange and bizarre, after he was found. He tried to climb the mountains six times. Finally, he disappeared completely. Gainsford says, "Here's my hope that Robert Conway will find his Shangri-La. Here's my hope that we all will find a Shangri-La."

The final scene shows Robert Conway breaking through the mountains to find Shangri-La again at last. The last scene is a shot of the set.

"*Lost Horizon*. I was proudest of that," said John Beckman in 1988.

Perhaps because he was able to depict for all the world a Shangri-La only verbalized by James Hilton in his novel. Perhaps because in the set designs Beckman was able to offer the best of our own civilization—an eclectic collection of Frank Lloyd Wright, Rembrandt, Chinese Chippendale, grand escaliers leading into plazas of the future, verdant trees, lovely parks, romantic lagoons with fountains, grillwork worthy of the best in Spain—magnificent images to satisfy any artist's ambition in scenic design.

Frank Capra found in this story a moral fable that has endured. It may seem utterly unrealistic to many, completely unattainable, but the utopian idea of a better society somewhere on this planet has had a lasting appeal, especially to the people before World War II in which Hitler and Hirohito would plunge the world into a holocaust of hate and destruction.

Everyone who worked on this memorable picture must ultimately have shared in the joy of creating a permanent monument through the transitory medium of film.

The Studios Then and Now

Production in Hollywood today (2006) is very complex and specialized, often divided among feature films for the large screen, television films, sitcoms, videos, talk shows, and radio broadcasting. What used to be exclusively film studios are often part of huge conglomerates, and, where the sound stage was once the primary locale for feature films, today motion pictures are shot in locations all around the world—for greater authenticity, of course.

Today's Hollywood also finds television production very much in the forefront, with HBO, PBS, and SHOWTIME especially prominent, as well as NBC, CBS, and ABC. Some movies are now made exclusively for television. Others appear to be made so that they can tap into the lucrative video rental market. So far as feature films for the big screen are concerned, independent production and distribution companies like Miramax/Weinstein, Lionsgate The Mirisch Corporation, New Line Cinema, Castle Hill, and Cannon have cropped up (and some have vanished), replacing the giant MGM-like studios that produced the major share of films in the 1930s and 1940s.

Actors, too, are more independent, often incorporating themselves as businesses and demanding salaries in the millions of dollars. Those who can do this are called superstars—Barbra Streisand, Bruce Willis, Sylvester Stallone, Tom Cruise, Jim Carrey. One successful picture at the box office can catapult even mediocre talent into instant stardom. Are they worth millions in salaries?

This wide-open field stands in marked contrast to the way things were done under the old studio system. Through the 1920s to the 1950s approximately, the studios were big corporations which signed actors to contracts (typically seven years) and then developed and nurtured their careers in a series of pictures designed to show them (or exploit them, if you will) to their best advantage. The actors had much less control of the material, except for the few like Bette Davis who could have a say in the final choice of other actors and the director for the film. The work, however, was secure and the work place familiar, something like an office or a home away from home to which you went day after day.

Occasionally things went wrong, such as when RKO ordered Katharine Hepburn to report for work on her next film, *Mother Carey's Chickens,* in the 1930s. Hepburn readily got the message that the studio (and through it the exhibitors) didn't think too much of her acting anymore, bought out the remainder of her contract, hightailed it to New York where she conned Philip Barry into writing *The Philadelphia Story* for her to do on the New York stage, made a success of that, bought the rights to the play and then sold them to MGM with herself as star, gaining a seven-year contract for herself, choice of leading men and director, making a resounding success of the film version of that play (1939), and following it up with her first successful teaming with Spencer Tracy in *Woman of the Year* (1942).

Another famous incident involved Olivia de Havilland in a suspension case at Warner Brothers. She wanted better roles and was put on a six-month suspension at the studio. When her contract expired, Warner Brothers claimed she owed them six more months for the length of the suspension.

She sued. The court ruled in favor of de Havilland, stating that seven years, including any suspensions, was the maximum limit of any studio contract. This has become known as the de Havilland statute in the industry.

Some actors who grew up in this studio system have claimed that the studios acted like giant parents or schools for them. The studio often did everything for its valued actors—educated them, covered for them in difficult social situations, photographed them only at their best, sent them lavish presents, and pampered them mercilessly.

But, at the same time, it could punish them if they misbehaved, sometimes with amusing results, such as when Louis B. Mayer wanted to teach bad boy Clark Gable a lesson and farmed him out to Poverty Row's Columbia, only to have Gable cop the Academy Award as Best Actor for the film he made there—*It Happened One Night* (1934).

MGM bounced Judy Garland out of *The Barkleys of Broadway* (1949) and brought in Ginger Rogers to replace her, and Garland again got the axe in *Annie Get Your Gun* (1950) with Betty Hutton getting the plum leading role.

When Bette Davis left Warner Brothers for good, after a stormy last few years there, Jack Warner is reported to have said, "Don't go. I've got a great property for you." "I'll bet it's a pip," shot back Davis. The hot property, of course, was *Gone With the Wind*, which he never made (David Selznick did), but, never mind, it was a nice idea.

It isn't just actors whose heads roll in the business. Executives, directors, scene designers, writers—everybody's job is always on the line. Julia Phillips wrote a bitter book about her experience in the film industry, *You'll Never Eat Lunch in this Town Again*.

Studio heads come and go. Louis B. Mayer's career ended sadly, as did Dore Schary's. Top-flight directors like William Wyler saw their work downgraded over the years. Father and son were pitted against one another in the Darryl Zanuck-Richard Zanuck struggle for control of 20th Century-Fox. Dave Begelman was thrown out for embezzlement and ended up a pathetic suicide.

Sherry Lansing, Dawn Steel, Barry Diller, Michael Eisner, Michael Ovitz, Marvin Davis, Robert Altman, Oliver Stone, Stanley Kubrick, Tom Rothman, Stacey Snider, Marc Platt—who's in? who's out?—do these names mean anything? The power shifts endlessly, sometimes subtly, othertimes like earthquakes.

John Jr. recalls the insecurities of growing up in the industry. He remembers people getting pink slips with their paychecks on Fridays. Workers didn't know whether they would have a job next week. John Jr. said many at Warner Brothers lived in this world of doubt. But he felt that his father worked with wonderful people in Warners' art department. He liked and respected his father's colleagues and said that they inspired him to go into architecture.

Today, new studios spring up regularly. Dreamworks, the most talked-about, was founded by a trio of talented men—Steven Spielberg, David Geffen, and Jeffrey Katzenberg, the new *wunderkinder* in town. Its plans showed how far-reaching its interests were. With two billion dollars as seed money and five hundred sixty employees, Dreamworks juggled CDs, feature films, and television sitcoms for eleven years.

But now Paramount/Viacom is absorbing DreamWorks, just as MGM was bought by the Sony Corporation. Production expenses are so inflated today that even the best independent companies have had to compromise quality in favor of money-making blockbusters, which, if they fail, can spell instant financial ruin for even those who care most for the movie industry.

The new Hollywood may be a puzzling maze, much like the freeway system that criss-crosses Los Angeles today, but the old Hollywood had its complexities too. A survey of the studio scene then might look something like the following.

Warner Brothers was a major film studio incorporated in 1923 in Burbank by Sam, Albert, Harry, and Jack Warner. It has always been located in Burbank, in the San Fernando Valley, where today, as part of the Time-Warner empire, it lies near Universal Studios in Universal City and the Walt Disney Studios.

This points up an interesting geographical fact: Many of the major studios never were physically situated in Hollywood, but were built in outlying areas. MGM (now Sony Studios) was in Culver City out toward Venice and Santa Monica. Twentieth-Century Fox was in West Los Angeles, and still is, although a major part of the old lot has been transformed into the Century City complex. Republic was in Studio City. United Artists had no studio of its own.

The major studios of Paramount, Columbia, Goldwyn, RKO, and the Chaplin Studios were, indeed, in Hollywood, as was most of the action before the 1920s. But when Warner Brothers presented the first talking picture, *The Jazz Singer* in 1927 with Broadway star Al Jolson in the leading role, change came roaring in swiftly, and Warner Brothers of Burbank was propelled into the front ranks of Hollywood studios.

Most people today think of Hollywood as being a state of mind, an attitude, a concept, rather than just a mere geographical locality anymore.

The big studios in the golden years of the 1930s and 1940s all had their particular styles. MGM, the most prestigious, had Clark Gable, Jeannette MacDonald, Nelson Eddy, Greta Garbo, Mickey Rooney, Judy Garland, and later, Katharine Hepburn and Spencer Tracy, among its stars.

It was known for lavish, opulent productions like those produced by Irving Thalberg for his wife, Norma Shearer—expensive, heavy, costume dramas like *The Barretts of Wimpole Street* (1934), *Romeo and Juliet* (1936), and *Marie Antoinette* (1938), although this latter film was produced by Hunt Stromberg and directed by W. S. Van Dyke, since Thalberg had died young in 1936.

When MGM undertook musicals, they were certain to be spectacular, like *Ziegfeld Girl* (1940), featuring Hedy Lamarr, Judy Garland, and Lana Turner, or the great Gene Kelly musicals, *On the Town* (1949), *An American in Paris* (1951), and *Singin' in the Rain* (1952), plus Fred Astaire and Judy Garland in *Easter Parade* (1948), a lavish remake of *Show Boat* (1951), and the winning *Seven Brides for Seven Brothers* (1954).

It was MGM who came up with the idea of Esther Williams in frothy bathing beauty musicals. They also produced Pearl Buck's drama about China, *The Good Earth* (1937), two literate Eugene O'Neill films, *Strange Interlude* (1932) and *Anna Christie* (1930), all the Mom-and-apple pie *Andy Hardy* films with Mickey Rooney, the *Dr. Kildare* series with Lew Ayres and Lionel Barrymore, the *Thin Man* series with Myrna Loy and William Powell.

Jean Harlow, Wallace Beery, Marie Dressler, and Joan Crawford (for the first part of her career) were MGM stars. Everything the studio touched tended to be big, wholesome, and impressive. This expensive ship of state was run by a paternalistic Louis B. Mayer for many years. Under his aegis, most of the definitive MGM quality films were made.

20th Century-Fox, another major studio, was the result of a merger between Twentieth Century and the Fox Film Corporation (founded in 1915). The two companies were merged in 1935 to become 20th Century-Fox, (so their logo read). Its films were bright, light-hearted, easy-going fare for moviegoers. Shirley Temple, Alice Faye, Don Ameche, Tyrone Power, Sonja Henie were its stars and its big money makers.

When Alice Faye left the studio after she married bandleader Phil Harris, the studio pushed Betty Grable into the limelight and brought on the Brazilian bombshell, Carmen Miranda, to delight audiences in zany, jazzy musicals.

Through the important years, Darryl Zanuck was the production chief. Marilyn Monroe was Fox's star of the 1950s in films like *The Seven Year Itch* (1955) and *Bus Stop* (1956).

In the 1970s, the studio had a major success with *Star Wars* (1977), but, today, filmmaking is only one part of Fox Inc., now run by publisher Rupert Murdoch. The other parts are Fox Television Stations, Inc., and Fox Broadcasting.

Paramount has a history that goes back to 1914. Its first major star was Mary Pickford, and the studio came about as the result of a merger between Adolph Zukor's Famous Players Film Company and the Paramount Pictures Corporation, founded by W. W. Hodkinson.

Paramount also took over the distribution of films made by Jesse L. Lasky's Feature Play Company, a corporation headed by Lasky, Samuel Goldwyn and Cecil B. DeMille, who produced *The Squaw Man* (1914), the first full-length feature motion picture ever produced, now the site of a museum in Hollywood.

Paramount, a highly eclectic studio, numbered among its stars Rudolph Valentino, Gloria Swanson, Mae West, Bing Crosby, Bob Hope, Dorothy Lamour, Alan Ladd, Veronica Lake, Burt Lancaster, Kirk Douglas, and Jerry Lewis over the years. But its dominant impression was probably made by the brilliant director, Cecil B. DeMille, and his enormous epics—*The Ten Commandments* (1923), *King of Kings* (1927), *Union Pacific* (1939), *Northwest Mounted Police* (1940), *Samson and Delilah* (1949), and *The Greatest Show on Earth* (1952).

Paramount also produced other quality films, like *The Heiress* (1949), *Sabrina* (1954), *Shane* (1953), a trio of Hitchock films—*Vertigo* (1958), *Psycho* (1960), and *Rear Window* (1954)— *Love Story* (1970), and both *Godfather* (1972, 1974) films.

They also produced such varied films as *Raiders of the Lost Ark* (1981), *Fatal Attraction* (1987*)*, *Ghost* (1990), and *Wayne's World* (1992*).* In an extremely involved history, Paramount was finally taken over by Gulf and Western, and then by Viacom where it, like 20th Century-Fox, is part of a conglomerate.

RKO, which stands for Radio-Keith-Orpheum, came out of a nickelodeon which became Mutual Film Corporation, and, finally, in 1928, RKO. Through the golden years its stars were Ginger Rogers, Fred Astaire, Katharine Hepburn, and Cary Grant.

Orson Welles brought his Mercury Theatre into an association with the studio and his memorable *Citizen Kane* (1941) was produced there.

Eccentric multimillionaire Howard Hughes nearly ruined the studio when he bought it, finally selling its assets to General Tire. The physical plant itself was bought in 1953 by a one-time contract player at RKO, Lucille Ball, and her husband, Desi Arnaz, and the studio renamed Desilu, producer of the hugely successful *I Love Lucy* television series.

United Artists was never a studio, but a producing, releasing, and distribution company for films by Charlie Chaplin, Mary Pickford, Douglas Fairbanks, and D. W. Griffith, who were its founders in 1919.

In the 1930s the high calibre films of Alexander Korda and Samuel Goldwyn appeared under the United Artists' banner. Later, United Artists released such films as *The African Queen* (1951), *Some Like It Hot* (1959), *Tom Jones* (1963), *One Flew Over the Cuckoo's Nest* (1975), *Rocky* (1976), and Woody Allen's *Annie Hall* (1977).

Suffering a fate similar to that of other studios, U.A. was sold to Trans-America, then in 1983 merged with MGM to become MGM/UA, and finally disappeared altogether when MGM/UA was bought by a French bank which renamed the whole operation Metro-Goldwyn-Mayer, Inc.

Universal is the film studio that, like the proverbial Phoenix, rises from the ashes. In Universal's case, it has risen at least twice. Founded in 1912 by Carl Laemmle, the company spread out onto its two hundred thirty acres in Universal City in the San Fernando Valley. Its triumphs in its early silent days were with Rudolph Valentino and Lon Chaney, "the man of a thousand faces," and then with the Bela Lugosi, Boris Karloff horror films, and a riveting production of *All Quiet on the Western Front* (1930).

Tottering on the brink of bankruptcy, the studio was saved by a young actress-singer, Deanna Durbin, in a series of musicals produced by Joe Pasternak that also helped promote classical music through films.

After Durbin's departure, Universal's fortunes were tied in with Abbott and Costello movies, Sabu, the elephant boy, Donald O'Connor, and Jeff Chandler.

Then Decca Records bought the controlling interest in Universal and the studio turned out the Doris Day-Rock Hudson comedies, until the 1970s, when they had several blockbuster movies, notably *The Sting* (1973), *American Graffiti* (1973), and *Jaws* (1975), directed by a young Steven Spielberg, who would then produce *E.T.* (1982) and *Jurassic Park* (1993), enormous moneymakers.

Added to this, is the physical building itself which, since the 1970s, has opened its doors to tours rivaled in popularity only by Disneyland in Anaheim, and then, in 1990, it opened the Universal Studios Theme Park in Orlando, Florida.

Along with this sideline, the studio continued producing top-level films like Kevin Costner's *Field of Dreams* (1989) and *Fried Green Tomatoes* (1991).

Columbia Pictures has had one of the most curious histories of any movie company. It began in 1920 when brothers Jack and Harry Cohn, together with Joe Brandt, founded the C.B.C/Film Sales Company, then incorporated themselves as Columbia Pictures in 1924. Nothing significant happened, however, until director Frank Capra came aboard and the astute Harry Cohn gave him *carte blanche* to create *It Happened One Night* (1934), *Mr. Deeds Goes to Town* (1936), *Lost Horizon* (1937), *You Can't Take It With You* (1938), and *Mr. Smith Goes to Washington* (1939).

In the 1940s, Columbia had a major star in Rita Hayworth and a big success with *The Jolson Story* (1946) and *Jolson Sings Again* (1949), but when Hayworth left to marry Prince Aly Khan, an angry Cohn tried to make an instant star out of Kim Novak, but it never really happened, although she added a pleasant, attractive presence to the films in which she appeared, notably *Picnic* (1956) and *Bell, Book, and Candle* (1958).

Since Columbia did not own any motion picture theatres, it didn't have to divest itself of them when the government cracked down in the 1950s on film studios that owned theatre chains that exhibited their films.

Columbia, also, was the first studio to jump into television with Screen Gems, through which they released their old films for television consumption.

Important Columbia feature films were *All the King's Men* (1949), *On the Waterfront* (1954), *The Bridge on the River Kwai* (1957), *Lawrence of Arabia* (1962), *Easy Rider* (1969), *Close Encounters of the Third Kind* (1977), and *Kramer Vs. Kramer* (1979), a respectable list on any studio's agenda.

But internal management problems and external take-over problems have taken their toll in recent years, making Columbia's story a tragi-comedy, at best.

Coca Cola bought the studio in 1982, sold it at a huge profit to Japan's Sony Corporation in 1989. Then, Coca Cola turned around with its TriStar Pictures and made a deal with Columbia to do business as Sony Pictures Entertainment. Sony today has taken over the old MGM studio in Culver City where it continues film and television production.

Minor studios in Hollywood of this period were Republic, founded in 1935, whose president, Herbert J. Yates, produced several films starring his wife, Vera Hruba Ralston, a Czechoslovakian ice-skating star, whom he tried to turn into a second Sonja Henie with no success, but he had greater luck with bland, routine westerns starring Gene Autry, Roy Rogers and Dale Evans. Republic no longer produced feature films in the 1950s when television became a more appealing outlet for its product.

Republic's rival in the western mode was Monogram, set up in 1930, and specializing in low-budget westerns featuring Tex Ritter, Tim McCoy, and others on its excellent ranch location. It also ground out the popular *Charlie Chan* series with Warner Oland and the *Bowery Boys* series. In 1946 it became Allied Artists Picture Corporation.

Certainly one of the most curious companies was Cosmopolitan Pictures, founded by William Randolph Hearst, to produce the films of his mistress, Marion Davies. With the Hearst Press to hype her films and Paramount Pictures to release them, from 1919 to 1923, Hearst pushed all the buttons, but all he and Davies ever achieved in this area was millions of dollars in debt.

Orson Welles used this debacle to telling effect in *Citizen Kane*, only he switched the locale from the film studio to the opera stage.

Into this kind of competition came the four Warner Brothers, yet they were not a singular overnight success with *The Jazz Singer* in 1927. Behind that, there were years of development and effort.

The brothers were Harry (1881-1958), Albert (1884-1967), Sam (1888-1927), and Jack (1892-1978). They founded the company as four brothers, but over the years death diminished their ranks until only one, Jack L. Warner, was left.

Their story seems typical of film pioneers. They were four sons in a family of twelve children who emigrated from Poland to the United States and settled finally in Youngstown, Ohio, where the father was alternately a butcher, a shoemaker, and the proprietor of a bicycle store.

In 1903, the enterprising father bought a nickel-odeon in Newcastle, Pennsylvania. Nickelodeons were jiffy movie theatres often set up in empty stores which charged a nickel for admission when the idea of moving pictures was catching on. As a diversion, live performers sometimes did their acts between the intermissions. In this one, Jack, who actually had been born along the way in Canada, sang and told jokes. The four brothers, trading on his talent and their interest, tried to break into the new industry, and finally in 1917 they established their studio in Burbank, California.

Jack, the one with the visible talent, was made production chief, the man responsible for the choice of scripts and the talent. Harry was made President, Albert became the treasurer, and Sam was the chief executive.

They gobbled up Vitagraph in 1925 and then First National Pictures, and began buying up theatre buildings to distribute their pictures. They owned their own theatre chain until the 1950s when government anti-trust suits forced them, and others, to sell their theatre holdings.

Although *The Jazz Singer* was a huge hit in 1927, the economic depression was just around the corner, and, more than any other studio, the Warner Brothers films reflected that period with some accuracy. The Brothers ran a tight ship and wanted no excessive frills in their pictures or anywhere around the studio.

When one thinks of the typical Warner Brothers movie of the period one thinks of stark, realistic depictions of situations in films like *I Am a Fugitive from a Chain Gang* (1932), *The Petrified Forest* (1935), *Kid Galahad* (1937), *Angels with Dirty Faces* (1938), *The Roaring Twenties* (1939), *They Made Me a Criminal* (1939), *The Fighting 69th* (1940), *They Drive by Night* (1940), *King's Row* (1942), and *All My Sons* (1948).

Warner Brothers always made an effort to import the best talent from the New York theatre. In *Blues in the Night* (1941), for example, one found Betty Field, Elia Kazan, and Richard Whorf, all very competent actors from the stage.

Kazan, a member of the Group Theatre (as was John Garfield), and later a director of the Actors' Studio in New York, would go on to become a highly regarded stage and film director. It was Kazan who directed one of his talented, yet unpredictable students, James Dean in Warner's *East of Eden* (1955). Dean's other two films *Rebel Without a Cause* (1955) and *Giant* (1956) were also produced by Warner Brothers. On these three films alone rests Dean's fame as a film legend.

Most of Bette Davis' important films were made at Warner Brothers, where she developed her high-tension acting style. She, Ida Lupino, and Olivia de Havilland were the reigning female stars there. The men were equally formidable—James Cagney, Errol Flynn, Humphrey Bogart, Edward G. Robinson, John Garfield, Claude Rains, and Paul Henreid.

Warner Brothers films were thoroughly grounded in realism and naturalism, meaning they were intensely believable. The social context was clear. Their films seemed relevant to real life, especially to middle-class people, and the writers and directors sought to provide strong sociological and psychological appeal.

Was there ever a more convincing murder film than Bette Davis and Gale Sondergaard in their dangerous cat-and-mouse game in Somerset Maugham's *The Letter*?

Why have audiences responded so strongly to Humphrey Bogart's movie persona as a tough guy? Or John Garfield's?

Why did Errol Flynn's swashbuckling films convince viewers that nobody was a more admirable hero than he?

Why did their film biographies of *Louis Pasteur* (1936), *Emile Zola* (1937), and *Juarez* (1939) bring history so vividly to life?

Because Warner Brothers hired no-nonsense directors, actors who could deliver, set designers who were artists, cinematographers who used the dispassionate camera lens properly, writers who could furnish a believable background for almost everything, and producers who agreed that every film they made should make a valid social comment, including musicals like the four *Gold Diggers* musicals (1929, 1933, 1935, 1937), *Footlight Parade* (1933), and *Go Into Your Dance* (1935) which aimed to provide some kind of gritty, realistic background for their otherwise routine show business stories.

John Beckman, with his rich, extensive background in art, travel, and practical experience in decoration, both in architecture and film, was now ready to join the art department of Warner Brothers full time where his talent would be recognized and he would be moved along until he became the ranking head art director there. But, first, a little sidetrack of some consequence.

Monsieur Verdoux

John Beckman's name first rolled across the screen in Charlie Chaplin's *Monsieur Verdoux* (1947), an unusual, controversial film released through United Artists. It's a tribute that the great comic genius, perhaps the most famous international film star there ever was, should have chosen Beckman to be art director for this ambitious film.

This picture also marked the first time Chaplin completely departed from his Little Tramp character, who had been half-present in his previous film *The Great Dictator* (1940) as the gentle barber in Tomania. That film, in which Chaplin also played a dictator named Hynkel (modeled on Adolph Hitler), had been roundly criticized for the actor's even attempting to play a character other than the beloved tramp, to whom audiences of all ages had responded so strongly over a long period of time.

To have the baggy-panted humanitarian completely absent in *Monsieur Verdoux* meant the film was destined to be denounced on that ground alone. But, typically, as in most of Chaplin's feature films, his pointed political satire also did not sit well with some in the United States, and that compounded the problem inherent in the reception *Monsieur Verdoux* received from critics and the public.

Charles Chaplin (1889-1977) was an Englishman who grew up working in the music halls with his half-brother Sydney Chaplin. The two worked in the Fred Karno troupe where Charlie developed extraordinary pantomimic skills.

The troupe appeared in the United States twice, in 1910 and 1912, and, from those performances, he was invited to join Keystone, a movie company run by

Mack Sennett in Burbank that specialized in comic films and became famous for its chases by crazy cops and its choruses of pretty bathing beauties. In one year, Chaplin made thirty-five films for Keystone, acting, directing, and writing.

In 1915, Charlie Chaplin signed with Essanay for more money and created *The Tramp* (1914) where his little man against the mean world was crystallized.

Then, in 1916, he joined Mutual, where he received ten thousand dollars a week, plus a huge bonus. Here he produced the hilarious short films, *Easy Street*, *The Adventurer*, *The Rink*, and *The Immigrant*.

In 1918, First National offered him a million dollars for eight two-reelers. *The Kid* (1921) with Jackie Coogan was the most acclaimed of these and brought him international attention.

In 1919, he joined D. W. Griffith, Mary Pickford, and Douglas Fairbanks in founding United Artists Corporation, which, from that point on, became Chaplin's primary releasing organization. *The Gold Rush* (1925), *The Circus* (1927), *City Lights* (1931), *Modern Times* (1933), and *The Great Dictator* (1940) are the result of that alliance.

Chaplin's attitude toward sound was always ambivalent, although he enjoyed writing the music for his films. *The Great Dictator* is the first film in which he really confronts the difficulties of using spoken dialogue, and, following that, in *Monsieur Verdoux*, he knew he had to use the human voice, and so he endowed Verdoux with his own rather patrician, educated English voice, which he as an actor had carefully trained throughout his years in show business. There was no trace of the struggle and poverty of his early years in his speech.

Like George Bernard Shaw, who was fifteen when he quit school, Chaplin was entirely a self-educated man who read serious literature, went to art galleries and museums, and asked the right questions, listening for answers along the way. His natural speaking voice, consequently, reflected his cultural interests.

Obviously, there was a lot of professional and political resentment against Chaplin's outspokeness and his ideas, especially those critical of the United States.

In 1952, when he and his wife were en route to Europe, the Attorney General revoked his right of re-entry to the U.S. unless he submitted to a close scrutiny of his life and views.

This was the deplorable Joseph McCarthy period in which that senator and his followers found communists everywhere, but most particularly in the film colony. Even zany comedienne Lucille Ball found her political views called into question. Xenophobic Americans in the film industry were especially resentful that Chaplin had never become a U.S. citizen since he had spent most of his life here and had made most of his money in Hollywood.

For the rest of Chaplin's life, Switzerland was to be his home.

He did receive honors in later life—from the Motion Picture Academy which awarded him an Oscar in 1972 for his life-long contributions to film. He returned to Hollywood for this ceremony and made a sweet reconciliatory speech.

In 1975, the Queen of England paid further tribute to him by knighting him Sir Charles Spencer Chaplin.

The films that he made late in life, *Limelight* (1952), *A King in New York* (1957), *The Countess from Hong Kong* (1967) are uneven in quality. Earlier movies like *The Gold Rush*, *City Lights*, and *Modern Times* are generally conceded to be his finest major works.

When John Beckman joined the *Monsieur Verdoux* group in 1944, he knew it would be a long shoot, since Chaplin always worked at a maddeningly slow pace, almost always over a period of several years before coming up with a finished product.

But Beckman also had the pleasure of working with several members of the Chaplin crew like film editor Willard Nico and cinematographer Roland (called "Rollie") Totheroh (1890-1967). Totheroh had begun at Essanay in 1910, met Chaplin there in 1915, and Chaplin insisted on his working with him on all his subsequent films. Sadly, *Monsieur Verdoux* was Totheroh's last film for his mentor.

The credits, as they rolled across the screen for *Monsieur Verdoux*, read:

Charles Chaplin

in

MONSIEUR VERDOUX

A Comedy of Murders
An original story written by
Charles Chaplin
Based on an idea by Orson Welles
featuring
Martha Raye

Director of Photography	Roland Totheroh
Operative Cameraman	Wallace Chewning
Art Director	John Beckman
Assistant Director	Rex Bailey
Film Editor	Willard Nico
Sound	James T.Corrigan
Artistic Supervisor	Curtis Courant
Wardrobe	Drew Tetrick
Make-up	William Knight
Hair Stylist	Hedvig Mjoral

Music Composed by
Charles Chaplin
Arranged and Directed by
Rudolph Schrager

Cast

Henri Verdoux alias Varnay alias Bonheur alias Floray	Charles Chaplin
Mona, his wife	Mady Correll
Peter, their son	Allison Roddan
Maurice Bottello, Verdoux's friend	ROBERT LEWIS
Martha, his wife	Audrey Betz

The Ladies

Annabella Bonheur	MARTHA RAYE
Annette, her maid	Ada-May
Marie Grosnay	ISOBEL ELSOM
Her maid	Marjorie Bennett
Yvonne, Marie's friend	HELENE HEIGH
Lydia Floray	Margaret Hoffman
The girl	Marilyn Nash

The Couvais Family

Pierre	Irving Bacon
Jean	Edwin Mills
Carlotta	Virginia Brissac
Lena	Almira Sessions
Phoebe	Eula Morgan

The Law

Prefect of Police	BERNARD J. NEDELL
Detective Morrow	CHARLES EVANS

Others in the Cast
WILLIAM FRAWLEY

Arthur Hohl	Barbara Slater
Fritz Leiber	Vera Marshe
John Harmon	Christine Ell

Lois Conklin

Associate Director
WHEELER DRYDEN
Associate Director
ROBERT FLOREY
Directed by
CHARLES CHAPLIN

The opening shot reveals a tombstone in a cemetery.
On it is written:

HENRI VERDOUX
1880-1937

We hear Verdoux's cultivated voice narrating, saying he was a bank clerk until the 1930 depression when he became unemployed. Then, he became a Bluebeard murderer of persons of the opposite sex so that he could support his suffering wife and child. "Only a person of undaunted optimism would have done this," he avers.

Cut to the home of the Couvais family in northern France. It appears to be a well-appointed house with typical middle class interior—many furnishings, credenzas, hutches with plates, dining room table with lace cover, brocaded fabric on dining room chairs. Piecrust tables are used generously. Tiffany lamps, anti-macassars, loveseat sofas, pillows, pictures, sconces on walls.

The family is talking about Thelma, who has run off to Paris to marry a man she's only known for two weeks. Thelma drew all her money out of the bank before she left.

Now the camera cuts to a small villa somewhere in the south of France. There's a long shot of a red-tiled house in the trees. We see an effete Monsieur Verdoux-Varnay, wearing a French beret and a smock, gardening. He enters his house. We see two graceful stair rails in the hall, where there is also an oval table. It is a light, airy, artistic-looking place. The room also has a low planter in it and a small oriental rug placed diagonally on the floor.

Verdoux-Varnay looks into a long looking glass, places a flower into a vase on the oval table.

The postman now arrives, bringing a registered letter for Thelma Varnay. Verdoux-Varnay pretends she's in the bathtub, and signs for her. The camera lingers on the graceful stair railing leading upstairs and on the French provincial moulding on the walls and doors.

Verdoux goes into the adjoining room, walks over to his desk. We see a piano, a table, the windows done in a light French provincial style.

He opens the letter. It says Thelma is the recipient of sixty-thousand francs which closes out her bank account. We see louvered doors in the room. Verdoux picks up the telephone, calls his broker, "Buy one hundred shares of Continental Copper!"

Cut to the Couvais family who are now seen in a law office, furnished with books and desks. We learn that twelve women have disappeared in the last few years. Apparently, there is a Bluebeard murderer on the loose who is also a bigamist.

The scene now shifts to a sign that says "House for sale." It is Varnay's house. Madame Grosnay, a prospective buyer, has come to look at it. We see the house through her eyes. We are in a large sitting room with wainscoting. There is a view of the hills from the window. We also see the garden.

Grosnay passes through the dining room, the library, and goes up to a bedroom which is sunny and boasts French screens. There is also a large triple-paneled pier glass. The walls have damask coverings on them.

Suddenly, Verdoux-Varnay appears in the house. He compulsively sniffs a rose. He is wearing a velvet smoking jacket and appears rather foppish. But he makes a crude play for Madame Grosnay, who is a large, elegant woman.

Cut to shot of a train. Then to Paris. Then to a boulevard. Then to a crowd of people. Then to exterior of a cafe with Verdoux sitting at a table outdoors. Verdoux buys a flower. Two men join him from his bank. He now gets up and leaves. One man says, after he has gone, "Poor old Verdoux. He was with us for over thirty years. Along came the depression. He was one of the first to go."

Verdoux now arrives at his home. He feeds the cat and enters the house. It is a huge antique gallery. We see massive Rodin-like sculptures, paintings, tapestries on the walls, antique French tables. A staircase leads up to a desk, fireplace, and ornate desk with a telephone on it. Verdoux's broker calls. The market is dropping. He needs fifty-thousand francs from Verdoux. Verdoux decides to call Lydia.

Cut to train moving. Then Verdoux, (as Monsieur Floray), pressing a tinkling door bell. Lydia answers. She is a shrew. You can tell by the way she's dressed. Black dress, brooch at throat. No make-up. Little old lady hair-do. Her house looks the same, very severe. Little round framed picture on wall looks like Lydia Pinkham. So does our Lydia.

Verdoux-Floray has been masquerading in this situation as an engineer in Indo-China.

While Lydia sits on a Victorian, tufted velvet love seat, he persuades her to withdraw money from the bank. In the room, we notice an interesting mirror over an elaborate fireplace. We see a Victorian gilded clock. There is a narrow staircase leading upstairs. Only one lighting sconce is seen. The window is plain.

Dissolve to the next morning. Verdoux emerges with the money box. He counts money. The kitchen is plain. The table has a simple checked table cloth on it. The hallway has narrow stairs with a drab tread carpet in the middle.

Cut to train in motion again. Camera focuses on a little boy, Jackie Cooper type, playing by a picket fence. Then a medium shot of his mother in a wheelchair. Peter is the boy's name. Mona is Verdoux's wife. They have been married ten years. As a wedding present, Verdoux gave her the deed to the house and garden. She says to him, "In the past three years, ever since you left the bank, you've been under a terrible strain." Verdoux tells her that millions of men are now unemployed, but that Mona and Peter are "all that I love on this earth."

Verdoux now sits in a huge wing chair. Peter playfully pulls the cat's tail. Verdoux reprimands him, saying, "You have a cruel streak in you. I don't know where you get it. Violence begets violence." We learn that the Verdoux family are vegetarians. We see Verdoux reading a newspaper with the headlines,

"WORLDWIDE DEPRESSION.
MILLIONS UNEMPLOYED."

It is too upsetting for Verdoux to continue. He puts down the newspaper.

Cut to Maurice Bottello arriving home with his wife, Martha. The decor in this house has a cathedral motif in the hutch, windows, and clocks. Plates are hung on the walls. Their front door has barn-like boards on the front door.

Cut to Verdoux traveling on the train again.

Cut to Annabella Bonheur (Martha Raye), dressed in an ostrich-plumed dressing gown. She emits a loud raucous laugh. In her house the decor is very frou-frou. There is a fringed shawl on a round table and, on the table, a vase containing cattails which thrust up into a stylized rectangular pattern. The windows are graced by swagged floor-length draperies. There is a fern on a high plant stand. Bibelots. Giddy, silly decor. Striped wallpaper.

Verdoux, in this house, masquerades as Captain Bonheur. He is seen arriving. As he enters, we notice an upright piano and a large, carved, upholstered Victorian sofa. The walls are hung with large paintings in ornate gilded frames. A Godey's *Ladies' Book* print is on the wall. There is painted wainscoting around the room. The clock on the mantel is a painted provincial one. Annabella wears a bizarre hat with what appear to be bouncing cherries or grapes in front.

Cut now to can-can dancers in what looks like a night club. The club is elaborate. There are etched glass doors, painted brick walls. Clustered white lights in little globes. Apparently Verdoux-Bonheur is a patron.

Cut to a pharmacist in his shop. We see Verdoux buying chloroform from him.

Cut to Annabella's boudoir. She has a huge brass and porcelain bed. The lampshades look like something from the 1920s. The draperies in this room are swagged shimmering ones.

Next scene is morning. The Bonheurs are having breakfast.

A succession of quick cuts from train to Paris to the art gallery office. Now a sign that reads, "151 Avenue Victor Hugo."

A flashback follows to a scene with Maurice and Martha, plus Henri Verdoux and wife Mona discussing lethal concoctions in a relaxed, conversational fashion.

Quick cuts again of train in motion to the Eiffel Tower in Paris to Henri Verdoux attempting a chemical experiment.

Cut to an Ingrid Bergman-like girl outside in the rain. She ducks into a doorway. Along comes Monsieur Verdoux who escorts her courteously under his umbrella. She has a kitten with her. He takes this poor girl to his apartment. We see a fireplace, bookcases full of books, an escritoire, a globe, an oil painting over the fireplace, a few vases.

Verdoux takes the bottle from the cabinet, intending to use the girl for his experiment. The girl is reading Schopenhauer. Verdoux, intrigued, asks her if she went to sleep wouldn't it release her from her horrible life? The girl says that life is wonderful. She explains that she was married once, but that her husband, an invalid, died. Verdoux thinks of his own incapacitated wife, Mona. The girl maintains that real love is sacrifice.

Verdoux persuades her to take a new glass of wine, and we see him deciding not to poison her after all. Instead, he gives her money. She cries.

Verdoux, who is wearing a grey fedora over his silver hair, tells her, "Don't believe too much. This is a ruthless world and one must be ruthless to cope with it."

She counters with, "That isn't true. This is a blundering world. Just a little kindness can make it beautiful."

"You'd better go before you corrupt me," Verdoux adds ruefully.

Cut to the flower shop. We see a detective whom we observe following Verdoux. Pan shot of Verdoux and crowd of people strolling along a boulevard.

Cut to Verdoux's apartment. Focus briefly on a round brass mirror like a bull's eye. Verdoux goes downstairs when Detective Morrow knocks at the door.

Morrow enters, comments on Verdoux's antiques. Verdoux points to one that looks like the statue of a saint. "This is rather amusing. An old galleon figure from the prow of a ship." We see a nude woman, a dressmaker's dummy.

Detective Morrow inquires about Thelma Varnay, Lydia Floray, Annabella Bonheur. The charges against Verdoux, he says, are bigamy and fourteen counts of murder. Verdoux asks to see his wife before being arrested.

Cut to Verdoux, handcuffed, with Detective Morrow, on a train. The detective had drunk some of Verdoux's tainted wine back at the apartment. Morrow dies on the train, and Verdoux escapes.

Cut to street scene. Verdoux and the girl. He gives her money, which she takes reluctantly. Verdoux appears sad to her eyes.

Cut to Verdoux who is seen experimenting with his poisons. He talks to Annabella and says he's coming home. We see a boat in drydock.

Train in motion again.

Annabella and Verdoux at home. Annabella in kitchen preparing dinner. Maid is excused. Verdoux hides poison in a peroxide bottle.

The maid drops the peroxide bottle. Takes the other bottle, which is really poison, to do her hair.

Verdoux pours peroxide into his wine bottle. He serves a glass of wine to Annabella. Nothing happens, of course. Instead, the glasses get switched. Verdoux discovers this, thinks he has poisoned himself. Meanwhile, the maid's hair starts to fall out. Annabella's pet name for Captain Bonheur is "pigeon," appropriately.

Cut now to a scene where a doctor is pumping out Verdoux's stomach. The doctor suggests that he and Annabella take a few days in the country.

The scene shifts now to a boat on a lake. Verdoux tries to lasso Annabella with an anchor on a rope. That doesn't work, so he tries to chloroform her, but the handkerchief lands on him while Annabella tries her hand at fishing. We hear and see yodelers in the distance who have field glasses and watch the scene.

Cut to Madame Grosnay's home. Grosnay is seen with her friend. Her home has elaborately rich decor. Verdoux-Varnay speaks to her on the telephone. Over her fireplace is a portrait of a woman, seated. Her glass cabinets are gilded; we see expensive objects inside.

In the next scene, we hear bells ringing. A wedding is to take place. The setting is a garden with a greenhouse and a conservatory.

We see Annabella Bonheur with one of the guests. Verdoux sees her also and bolts behind the lattice outside the greenhouse. Inside there is a long table with a cloth, champagne, etc. Verdoux crawls under the table. Then Verdoux runs away.

Cut to a law office. All the women are now telling their stories. "He told Grosnay he was an explorer," etc. A confidential investigation is launched.

Cut to newspaper headlines reading "STOCK MARKET CRASHES. BANKS FAIL." We see a man shooting himself and another jumping out the window of a skyscraper.

Quick cut to Verdoux on the phone, telling his broker he is wiped out.

Headlines again:

"CRISIS IN EUROPE.
HITLER. MUSSOLINI. NAZIS BOMB SPANISH
LOYALISTS."

Cut to a shot of Verdoux walking. An expensive car pulls up. The woman in the car beckons him to her. The girl, rich now, looks like Barbara Hutton. She puts him into her chauffeured car. "To the Cafe Royale." She explains that she met a munitions manufacturer.

The scene now is the Cafe Royale—-a ballroom with tango dancers. The rich girl and Verdoux.

Verdoux says, "Everyone needs love. . . . Soon after the crash I lost my wife and child . . . . since the loss of my family I seem to have awakened from a dream. I was a bank clerk once . . . . a moment of confusion, a nightmare, in which I lived in a half-dream world. . . . Despair is a narcotic that lulls the mind into indifference."

The girl replies, "We must go on if only to fulfill our destiny."

Now Verdoux-Floray's shrewish wife, Lydia spots him. We notice the chandelier, the beautiful glass doors in the ballroom set.

Cut to exterior of Cafe Royale. Verdoux has locked Lydia into a room. He tells the rich girl, "I'm going to fulfill my destiny."

The detectives who have been tailing him inside the Cafe Royale now exit. Comic confusion ensues in which Verdoux joins the seekers and peers in on the scene as they nab the wrong man.

Back to the traveling train scene again.

Cut to the trial by jury in a law court. Gendarmes. The prosecutor wants death on the guillotine. Verdoux is found guilty.

Verdoux states that, for thirty-five years, he used his brains honestly. "But the world builds mass engines of destruction for killing. The world encourages mass murder and does it very scientifically. As a mass murderer, I'm an amateur by comparison. I shall see you all very soon, very soon."

Cut to reporters outside Verdoux's cell. "No pictures." Verdoux is lying down on his cot in the cell. His lawyer talks to him. "That's the history of many a big business—wars, conflict. Numbers sanctify."

A priest now appears. In the jail cell now, the priest and Verdoux are alone. Verdoux confronts the priest, "What would you do without sin?" Verdoux lifts up a glass of rum and defiantly swallows it. Then he goes with the men to the guillotine. He walks down a long hall toward a Romanesque oval door.

The End

The problem with this material is that it is not particularly funny. Chaplin's Bluebeard lacks charm. Why he elected to make him foppish is a mystery. He occasionally endows him with the Little Tramp's gallantry toward women, but the idea of a man's being a bigamist and a mass murderer is scarcely amusing, hardly what audiences expected from the world's most beloved comic actor.

It's interesting that Orson Welles, another great nay-sayer, suggested the whole idea to Chaplin. Perhaps this indicates that it would have been a better film had Welles made it instead of Chaplin.

The heavy-handed, stifling infusion of Schopenhauer's life-is-a-nightmare philosophy also was scarcely a laughing matter to audiences. Nor the rich-man-poor-man ideas borrowed from Shaw. Not even the grotesque parody of Dreiser's *An American* Tragedy is particularly funny.

But the major problem with the theme was its simplistic idea that capitalism makes ordinarily nice people into mass murderers—in this case, not really proved thematically, not really relevant to real life, and, again, not made amusing in this movie.

The sets by John Beckman are always interesting, forming a complementary background to Verdoux and his various women, and the music (by Chaplin) also supports the actors nicely.

But it is hard to laugh at this particular fable, and *Monsieur Verdoux* remains one of Chaplin's most perplexing creations—although certainly not without high marks for its stab at being different, well noted by the Academy in 1947 when they gave Chaplin a nomination for "best original screenplay." Even more to the Academy's credit— he didn't win.

John Beckman's famous patience was tried to the fullest on this film for which he worked very hard. He regarded Chaplin as "very pleasant, very courteous" to work with.

He had, indeed, helped Chaplin out in a personal way at the beginning of this film in 1945 when he designed a nursery for Chaplin and Oona O'Neill Chaplin's daughter, Geraldine, for their Summit Drive residence in Beverly Hills. This residence for years was called "Chaplin's Folly" by industry wags because Chaplin had it built and furnished by all the people with whom he worked in the industry. Movie sets are not made to last a lifetime, are they? Constantly in need of repair, "Chaplin's Folly" at least gave additional employment to his colleagues.

For Beckman, however, Chaplin gave him his name in the credits on the screen, and that couldn't have been a greater gift, because the studio for whom Beckman had been working, Warner Brothers, finally noticed him, rewarding him by promoting him to fully accredited Art Director.

John Beckman's name, from that point on, would appear in the credits on every film he did.

The Warner Brothers Years

In 1948 there was a brief moment when the major film studios held their breath because of the onslaught of television. The studios, downsizing, closed their doors for about six months.

John Gabriel Beckman's friend, Harry Hall, the man who had originally encouraged him to move to Los Angeles, got him work with an architectural firm to tide him over until more work became available. Hall was now the chief draftsman for Gordon Kaufman, well-known architect, and he was instrumental in getting Beckman a job as contact man or project manager. Beckman did the program for the new geology building at U.C.L.A.

But then, the action picked up again at the studios and Beckman went back to work in films. However, after that point, architectural firms in Los Angeles were reluctant to hire anyone from the studios because of Beckman's walking out on them.

From 1948 to 1970, John Gabriel Beckman worked primarily at Warner Brothers as a credited art director. He did twenty films for Warner Brothers, but also was art director for *Wake Me When It's Over* (1960) at Fox, *The Devil at Four O'Clock* (1961), *Who's Minding the Mint?* (1967), *Hook, Line, and Sinker* (1969), at Columbia, and *In Enemy Country* (1968) at Universal.

The principal director on whose team he was an integral part was Mervyn LeRoy, for whom he did ten films altogether.

Mervyn LeRoy (1900-1987) was associated with two of the major studios—Warner Brothers and MGM—and did almost totally different kinds of work at each. He and John Beckman shared something in common: Both were survivors of the San Francisco earthquake of 1906.

LeRoy had been born in that city, and, because his father's department store had been destroyed, he became a newsboy at age ten, and then became an actor at twelve as a newsboy in a production of *Barbara Fritchie.*

He moved from there into vaudeville where his diminutive size and good tenor voice helped his burgeoning acting career. Luckily, he had a cousin, Jesse L. Lasky, in the business in Hollywood, who got him a job folding costumes at Famous Players-Lasky. Luckier still for his career later on, he married Harry Warner's daughter, Doris, who became his second wife.

From costumes to bit parts to gag writer to writer, LeRoy worked his way up until, in 1927, he began directing for Warner Brothers/First National. He actually helped shape the typical social dramas for which Warner Brothers became renown in the 1930s. LeRoy directed Edward G. Robinson in the powerful *Little Caesar* (1931), and, in the next year, Paul Muni in *I Am a Fugitive from a Chain Gang* (1932).

But a major key to LeRoy's technique was versatility. He directed the sparkling *Gold Diggers of 1933* with Dick Powell, Ruby Keeler, and Ginger Rogers, and, for MGM, the classic *Tugboat Annie* (1933) with Wallace Beery and Marie Dressler.

From 1938 until the mid 1950s, he worked at MGM, directing mostly vehicles for stars such as *Waterloo Bridge* (1940) for Vivien Leigh, *Random Harvest* (1942) and *Madame Curie* (1943) for Greer Garson, *Thirty Seconds Over Tokyo* (1944) for Spencer Tracy and Van Johnson, and *Quo Vadis* (1951) for Robert Taylor and Deborah Kerr.

Sometimes he produced, as well as directed. The classic *The Wizard of Oz* (1939) was produced by him; the director was Victor Fleming. All his MGM films were of a very high order.

In 1955, he co-directed *Mister Roberts* with John Ford (who was ill) for Orange/Warner Brothers, and then moved over to that studio completely to finish out his career with *Mary, Mary* (1963).

He had one last film to direct, at Universal, the ill-fated bomb *Moment by Moment* (1965) with Lily Tomlin and John Travolta, an ironic way to end a distinguished career.

He had received a special Academy Award for his documentary *The House I Live In* (1945) and was awarded the prestigious Irving Thalberg award for his total achievement in film (1975).

John Beckman actually first worked for Mervyn LeRoy as a set designer at Warners in 1938 on a film called *Fools for Scandal* which had Beckman's friend, Anton Grot as art director, Ted Tetzlaff as the cinematographer, and Carole Lombard, Ralph Bellamy, and Fernand Gravet in the cast.

This film, hoping to capitalize on Lombard's skills as a sophisticated comedienne, jumps from Hollywood to Paris to London, with Lombard portraying Kay Winters, a movie star, who gets involved with a penniless French marquis René, (played by Gravet), who poses a threat to insurance man Ralph Bellamy for Kay's affections.

René poses as a butler and cook in Kay's household, protecting her from the contamination of the insurance man, until true love wins out, because, presumably, the charm of René and the romantic aura of life in Paris are too much for anybody, let alone Kay, to resist.

Grot, Beckman, and company provide the requisite glamorous background for these proceedings, and even Richard Rodgers and Lorenz Hart added a few musical ditties.

In 1956, when LeRoy switched back to Warner Brothers from MGM, Beckman was hired by him to be art director on *The Bad Seed*, with Hal Rosson as cinematographer, and a cast including Nancy Kelly, Patty McCormack, and Eileen Heckart.

This film, a psychological horror story, scored big in its day, scaring audiences with its story of a young girl who becomes an easy murderer because a schoolmate won a prize she had coveted.

John Beckman was able to take ordinary objects, like pieces of furniture—beds in a room, for example—and make them appear slightly sinister in their designs.

Hal Rosson, the photographer, then photographed them with expressionistic lighting so that they looked even more threatening. The film was directed by LeRoy with the mounting suspense that plays well on the large screen because of its enormous magnitude. The three actresses all received Academy Award nominations for their performances, and Hal Rosson one for his cinematography.

Harold (Hal) Rosson (1895-1960) started his film career as a camera operator in 1913 and soon became an important cameraman, working primarily on MGM productions like *Captains* Courageous (1937), *The Wizard of Oz* (1939), and *Singin' in the Rain* (1952).

He also was the last husband of one of its stars, Jean Harlow, and received an Academy Award for his Technicolor achievements in *The Garden of Allah* (1936).

Two of Rosson's most distinguished films were *The Asphalt Jungle* (1950) and *The Red Badge of Courage* (1951), both directed by John Huston for MGM.

In 1956, the LeRoy-Beckman-Rosson team undertook a fascinating project for William Holden who had just formed the Toluca Company for production of films. *Toward the Unknown* was an action-adventure epic in color (Warner-scope and Warner Color) that featured Holden as Major Lincoln Bond, a test pilot in the U.S. Air Force.

With exciting scenes shot on location at Edwards Air Force Base, including aerial acrobatics by the U.S.A.F. Thunderbirds, Beckman and Rosson were able to give it an authentic, believable environment, although audiences are likely to remember most the sensational special effects and the Thunderbirds.

Home Before Dark (1958) was another highly successful Mervyn LeRoy film from the 1950s. English actress Jean Simmons was the star, playing a woman who has returned from a hospital, where she was treated for mental illness, to her New England home, where her unloving husband, stepmother, and stepsister allegedly help her recover.

The film, viewed from Simmons' point of view, offered Beckman and the cinematographer (Joseph Biroc), the opportunity to twist scenery and viewpoint artistically, so that, a long hospital corridor becomes, to Simmons, something frightening and dungeon-like, reminiscent of the stunning expressionistc scenes in Orson Welles' *Citizen Kane*.

The photographer on this film, Joseph Biroc (1903-1996), unlike Hal Rosson, began his career later in life. He had been with the U.S. Army Signal Corps in World War II, and had beautifully captured the liberation of Paris on film for them. The jump into commercial film was an easy one for him.

He gained acclaim for himself by photographing the first 3-D film, *Bwana Devil* (1953). Other films he photographed included *Viva Las Vegas* (1964), *Hush, Hush, Sweet Charlotte* (1965), *Escape from the Planet of the Apes* (1971), *The Towering Inferno* (1974), and *Airplane* (1980). He received an Oscar for his work on *The Towering Inferno*, plus a Life Achievement Award from the Society of American Cinematographers in 1989.

Mervyn LeRoy and John Beckman tackled two challenging Rosalind Russell vehicles for Warner Brothers—*A Majority of One* (1961) and *Gypsy* (1962).

This time, they used as cameraman, Harry Stradling, Sr. (1902-1970). Born in England, Stradling moved to the United States when young, where he worked as a cameraman on Hollywood films from 1920 until 1929. Then he was a cameraman in France, notably on *Carnival in Flanders* (1935), followed by a stint in England on *Pygmalion* and *The Citadel* (both 1938) and *Jamaica Inn* (1939).

Back in Hollywood from 1940 to 1970, Stradling's most memorable films included Alfred Hitchcock's *Suspicion* (1941), *The Human Comedy* (1943), *Easter Parade* (1948), *A Streetcar Named Desire* (1951), *Guys and Dolls* (1955), *Auntie Mame* (1958), *Who's Afraid of Virginia Woolf?* (1966), *Funny Girl* (1968), and *Hello Dolly* (1969). He died while filming *The Owl and the Pussycat* (1970). Andrew Laszlo completed the photography on this film.

The sets, costumes, and makeup for *A Majority of One* were unusual. The locales ranged from Brooklyn to a ship at sea to Japan.

Rosalind Russell portrayed a middle-aged Jewish woman and Alex Guinness played a Japanese gentleman. The two of them become involved in a charming relationship with, quite naturally, international moral overtones. Russell and Guinness, skilled at hilarious comic characterizations, carried them off triumphantly, Russell especially, since she was playing a role created by the brilliant actress Gertrude Berg on the stage and closely identified with her personality.

In *Gypsy*, Rosalind Russell again took on a formidable task, now playing Mama Rose, a role created by the dynamic Ethel Merman on the Broadway stage.

Beckman's job here was to conjure up the early days of vaudeville and burlesque, making them seem authentic, yet appealing, and to up-date the sets chronologically until we reach the present-day world of show business.

Again, Beckman, Mervyn LeRoy, and company came through handsomely. Despite a certain conservative hesitation not to stray too far from the original material, the film garnered three Academy Award nominations.

Beckman's assignment on *The F.B.I. Story* (1959), with Mervyn LeRoy directing and Joseph Biroc on camera was also well received. James Stewart plays an F.B.I. agent with principles, naturally, in this one, married to Vera Miles. The story follows his professional life as a crime-fighter over the years and offers an exciting chase scene through the streets of New York City. The sets and story are convincingly realistic, as is the acting of Miles and Stewart.

In 1960, Mervyn LeRoy made a film at Fox, *Wake Me When It's Over*, and took John Beckman with him to this studio to be art director and Joseph Biroc to be cinematographer. This film was a comedy tailored to the talents of Ernie Kovacs, and also featured the hi-jinks of Dick Shawn and Don Knotts.

The story seems to be a comic re-telling of *The Teahouse of the August Moon*, with Shawn as an army veteran who plans to build a resort hotel on the Pacific island, Shima, where there is a radar station whose commandant is Ernie Kovacs. Shawn has his eye on all the surplus material.

The hotel gets built, the islanders all get work as waiters, busboys, etc., everything appears happy and prosperous, but an unfortunate lie is spread about the situation on the island, so that a senator in Washington, D.C. launchs a Congressional investigation, leading to a court martial of Dick Shawn, who, it turns out, isn't even in the army anymore.

In 1961, Mervyn LeRoy again jumped ship at Warner Brothers, this time to Columbia to make *The Devil at Four O'Clock*, with his team of Beckman and Biroc.

The Devil at Four O'Clock was an adventure in itself for John Beckman, since the movie was filmed on the island of Maui in Hawaii (standing in for a South Pacific island here called "Kalua") and its stars were Spencer Tracy and Frank Sinatra.

Tracy played an alcoholic priest who, along with three convicts, saves the lives of some leprous children who need to be rescued from their hospital high up on a mountain when a volcano erupts.

The volcanic conflagration in which the entire island disappears into the ocean is a central attraction in the film. Both Biroc and Beckman had a field day with the exotic locale, as did Tracy and Sinatra with their unusual roles.

Mary, Mary (1963) was Mervyn LeRoy's farewell to Warner Brothers and the last film John Beckman and Harry Stradling, Sr. would work on with him.

This screenplay by Richard Breen, from the Broadway stage play by Jean Kerr, is a smart New York City comedy about the publishing and literary world and starred Debbie Reynolds and Barry Nelson as an ex-married couple who ultimately get back together only after the usual complications, provided by another man and another woman, plus a dramatic New York snowstorm that becomes a participant in the plot itself.

John Beckman worked with directors other than Mervyn LeRoy during his Warner years. Two of the best were William Wellman and Michael Curtiz.

Lafayette Escadrille (1958) was the last film directed by the legendary William Wellman. Since the film had a military setting, Beckman probably was given this assignment because of his work on William Holden's air force film *Toward the Unknown*.

It is appropriate that Wellman ended his career with *Lafayette Escadrille* because he co-wrote the screenplay, with the material coming out of his own life story. William Wellman (1896-1975) was one of Hollywood's most famous directors of men's stories, and a legend for the fistfights, wild parties, and other off-screen shenanigans that colored his work.

In 1913, he was a professional ice hockey player. In 1917, he joined the French Foreign Legion, where he flew planes under the aegis of the Lafayette Escadrille.

Then, in 1918, Wellman began his film career, at first acting, then becoming an assistant director, until he lucked out in 1927, when he directed *Wings*, the first film ever to win an Academy Award as Best Picture. He also picked up another Oscar as co-writer of *A Star Is Born* (1937), and, over the years, directed such powerful films as *The Call of the Wild* (1935), *Beau Geste* (1939), *The Ox-Bow Incident* (1943), *The Story of G.I. Joe* (1945), and *Battleground* (1949).

But it is Wellman's work at Warner Brothers in the early 1930s that many audiences and critics remember most. He directed *The Public Enemy* (1931), for example, famed for the scene in which James Cagney smashes a grapefruit into Mae Clarke's face, and for the socio-psychological background, so typical of Warners' gangster films of this period.

Cagney played Tom, a tough hoodlum who grows up from 1909 to 1920 in the film, along with his buddy Matt, played by Edward Woods. They encounter brassy dames like Joan Blondell and Jean Harlow, as well as Mae Clarke, in their adventures.

Wellman is able to endow this material with enough intelligence to try to get at its roots, so that audiences have an understanding of why a policeman got killed and why Tom and Matt behave in their anti-social way. It also established James Cagney's pugnacious screen persona for his early films.

Lafayette Escadrille starred another tough guy, Clint Eastwood, early in his film career, paired opposite sensitive guy Tab Hunter, in a typical survival story, so characteristic of Wellman's work, and, apparently, his own life.

On this film, Beckman worked with cinematographer William M. Clothier (1903-1996), the favorite cameraman of directors Wellman and John Ford, and also the actor, John Wayne. Clothier had begun his career at Warner Brothers in 1923 as a set painter. Then he became an assistant cameraman, providing the classy aerial photography for Wellman's *Wings* in 1926.

During World War II, Clothier flew twenty-five combat missions over Germany with the 8th Air Force. He excelled in outdoor color photography. He retired from the industry after filming John Wayne's *The Train Robbers* in Mexico in 1972.

1959 found John Beckman working once again with one of Warner Brothers' most charismatic directors, Michael Curtiz, on *The Helen Morgan Story* (1959).

Michael Curtiz (pronounced ker-TEEZ) was the anglicized name of Mihaly Kertesz (1888-1962), an Hungarian who began his career as the first prominent director of Hungarian films with *Az utolso bohem* and *Ma es holnap* (both 1912), then moved on to Denmark, Sweden, France, Germany, and Austria, gaining fame for the two-part *Sodom und Gomorrah* (1922, 1923), before coming to Hollywood in 1926 to work for Jack Warner.

Curtiz had studied at Markoszy University and the Royal Academy of Theatre and Art in Budapest, and had begun his career as an actor on the stage. In addition, he was a thoroughly professional, equable director with special expertise on European culture, not overlooked by Warner in the assignments and actors sent Curtiz's way.

Michael Curtiz was the director Jack Warner paired up with Errol Flynn in ten pictures, including *Captain Blood* (1935), *The Charge of the Light Brigade* (1936), The *Adventures of Robin Hood* (1938), *The Private Lives of Elizabeth and Essex* (1939), *The Sea Hawk* (1940), and *The Sea Wolf* (1941).

Guiding the swashbuckling action-adventure hero, Errol Flynn, through his greatest films was perhaps Curtiz's strongest contribution to the studio, but audiences and film historians will always remember him as the director of *Casablanca* (1942), with Ingrid Bergman, Humphrey Bogart, and Paul Henreid locked in an international triangle.

Sometimes overlooked is Curtiz's direction of James Cagney in *Yankee Doodle Dandy* (1942), Bing Crosby and Danny Kaye in *White Christmas* (1954),

Elvis Presley in his strongest film *King Creole* (1958), and Joan Crawford in her Academy-Award winning performance in *Mildred Pierce* (1945), as well as in *Flamingo Road* (1949).

Michael Curtiz received an Academy Award as Best Director for *Casablanca*.

John Beckman worked with Michael Curtiz on six films, including *Casablanca* and *Mildred Pierce*.

On *Casablanca*, when art director Carl Jules Weyl became ill, Beckman finished out the film for him, providing the famous final scene at the airport where Rick and Ilsa say goodbye to each other.

On *Mildred Pierce*, Anton Grot was the credited art director, providing his typical sinister, Gothic look to ordinary settings to heighten the mystery. Beckman worked with him on this slightly distorted, expressionistic look. The film, including Crawford's brilliant performance, is a masterpiece of the *film noir* genre.

The Helen Morgan Story (1959), however, with Curtiz directing, Beckman as art director, and Ted McCord, as cinematographer, seems only a routine effort. Stars Ann Blyth, Paul Newman, and Richard Carlson can do little more with a weak script than look decorative.

Perhaps the famed torch singer's life wasn't as interesting as the producer had thought, or maybe it required a totally different approach. The film, with its show business and night club background, has very little bite to it and offers few new insights into Helen Morgan's life.

Two Doris Day films, *By the Light of the Silvery Moon* and *Calamity Jane* (both 1953) added another feather to Beckman's cap professionally, for the star was just making her mark as a movie star after years as a successful singer. Both films were directed by David Butler with Wilfrid M. Cline as photographer.

David Butler (1894-1979) was a Stanford educated man whose father had been a stage director. David himself was on stage at age three and appeared in some of D. W. Griffith's films and in *Seventh Heaven* (1927), which won Janet Gaynor the first ever Academy Award for an actress.

In 1927, Butler began directing films for Fox and was known throughout his long career, first as the director of the great Shirley Temple movies *Bright Eyes* (1934), *The Little Colonel* and *The Littlest Rebel* (both 1935), and *Captain January* (1936), and then as the director of other light-hearted, charming musicals like *Road to Morocco* (1942), *Shine on Harvest Moon* (1944), and *Where's Charley?* (1952)

It was a good thing for John Beckman to have worked on these two movies during the preceding year, 1952, because his wife Nellie had died in December, 1951 of a heart attack brought on after a diagnosis of cancer. Inwardly, he felt very lost without Nellie, but, typically, he said little and kept himself occupied with his busy schedule at the studio.

Luckily, he met a charming woman named Layne Grey who was Doris Day's stand-in for *By the Light of the Silvery Moon*, and one day he decided to ask her to his house to meet his son and to get further acquainted.

"Would you cook a nice dinner if I bring someone home?" John asked his son mysteriously.

"Yes," replied John, Jr. And he did, preparing a steak dinner so carefully that dinner wasn't served until 11:00 p.m., John Jr. being unaware that, because of Layne's hypoglycemic condition, she had to eat dinner promptly at 7:00 p.m. each night.

Despite that, Layne and John fell in love, and, about a week later, both Beckmans went to meet Layne's parents, and then, shortly after, Layne and John were married in a beautiful, simple ceremony.

So the two Doris Day movies brought him personal happiness, as well as professional. On June 21, 1954, Layne and John's daughter Jane was born. They were living in Sherman Oaks at the time, but would later buy a large trailer and move up to Avila Beach in San Luis Obispo County in 1962, the same year in which John Beckman had a heart attack in March.

He and Layne subsequently bought a home in Cambria in that same year, and John became a commuter, spending week days down in Hollywood working, and staying at the Sherman Oaks house, and then returning to Cambria for the week ends.

In 1967, the Beckmans would open an antique shop in Cambria which they ran until 1973, when they closed it. But that's getting ahead of the story.

Several other of Beckman's Warner Brothers films deserve mention here. One is *Springfield Rifle* (1952), notable for its taciturn star, Gary Cooper, and its director, the mercurial Andre de Toth (1910-2000).

Like Michael Curtiz, Andre de Toth was Hungarian. He studied law at the University of Budapest, but joined a theatre group in 1926. He began in film as a writer and editor, actor, and director. When war broke out in 1939, he went to the front as a correspondent, and then emigrated to England where he worked for Alexander Korda (also of Hungarian origin) on such films as *Four Feathers* (1939), *The Thief of Bagdad* (1940), and *The Jungle Book* (1942).

In 1953, de Toth directed a 3-D film, *House of Wax*, for Warner Brothers, which brought him some attention for his skill in scaring an audience. In several of his early films he showed a knack for psychological melodramas with a *film noir* slant in which he would plunge a leading character into the middle of events from which there seemed no escape—*Dark Waters* (1944), for example, in which Merle Oberon tries to untangle her muddled past in the bayoux of Louisiana, *Guest in the House* (1944), where Anne Baxter plays an emotionally disturbed young woman who feels trapped in an otherwise normal home, and *Pitfall* (1948), in which Dick Powell inadvertently gets caught up in a murder and finds himself in a no-win situation.

De Toth was much admired for his brilliant use of peripeties in film. These plot-twists, or reversals in fortune, were first discussed by Aristotle in his *Poetics* and have been an essential part of dramas, especially suspenseful ones, ever since. Sometimes they are called switcheroos. The audience expects something to happen in the story, only it doesn't; the opposite happens, so the audience keeps watching, like a cat watching a mouse, to see what will occur next. De Toth seems to have viewed life as essentially that—tricks—a now-you-see-it-now-you-don't world of distrust and deception.

The other genre de Toth was successful at directing was the Western. *Man in the Saddle* (1951), *Carson City* (1952), *Springfield Rifle* (1952), *The Bounty Hunter* (1954), *The Indian Fighter* (1955) are all his work.

De Toth was co-author of the screenplay for *The Gunfighter* (1950) and won an Academy Award nomination for his script. Again, a hero in an impossible situation, fighting for his life in a vicious environment, appears to have attracted his interest. One might call him a survivalist director.

In private life, Andre de Toth was known as the moody director whose first wife was the pixyish Veronica Lake.

During the 1960s, de Toth directed television episodes of *Bronco, Maverick, The Westerner,* and *77 Sunset Strip.* He also directed some films in Europe. His vision may have been too cynical, his world too dark and cruel, for American audiences of the time.

Another of Beckman's Warner films was *Hell on Frisco Bay* (1956), a collaboration between Alan Ladd's Jaguar Films and Warner Brothers. This film was directed by Frank Tuttle who had directed Ladd in his first hit, *This Gun for Hire* (1942), at Paramount.

Ladd showed Hollywood loyalty when he hired Beckman who had worked with him as art director on *The Iron Mistress* (1952) and also John Seitz, who had done the same, as cameraman, even though Seitz was sixty-three years old and not in good health at the time.

Hell on Frisco Bay was an action-crime drama in which Alan Ladd, as Steve Rollins, is a former policeman, wrongly accused of a crime, who has just been released from prison. He vows to get the man who framed him, and this takes him to Warner's leading gangster actor, Edward G. Robinson, who, in this film, has Mafia connections. The complications include the requisite thrilling chase across San Francisco Bay after which Steve Rollins is eventually reconciled with wife Marcia, played by Joanne Dru.

John Beckman's last feature film for Warner Brothers was a Jerry Lewis comedy, *Which Way to the Front?* (1970). The previous year, Beckman had been the art director for *Hook, Line, and Sinker,* which

George Marshall had directed, with Jerry Lewis as star, for Columbia. In this film, Peter Lawford plays Jerry Lewis' family doctor who tells him he has only a few months to live because of his heart condition.

Lewis' wife (played by Anne Francis) suggests he go fishing around the world, which he does, until the doctor catches up with him in Portugal and says his diagnosis was wrong and that he should stage his own death so that his wife can collect his hefty insurance policy.

The doctor says that, after seven years, Lewis can return to his wife, the joke being that the doctor and the wife have planned the whole thing, including Lewis' real death, after which they will live happily and wealthily together.

Which Way to the Front?, on the other hand, was both produced and directed by Jerry Lewis. In it, Lewis is a rich man who is 4-F during World War II, but, patriotically, he gets together a little army of his own and goes to Italy, intending to kidnap a Nazi general. Lewis disguises himself as the Nazi general at one point, getting himself into hot water with the Allies. This is somewhat like Charlie Chaplin's *The Great Dictator* in its attempt to demonstrate Lewis' comic genius.

At least, *Which Way to the Front?* gave John Beckman the chance to come up with some kooky army vehicles to use in the film.

Layne Beckman said Jerry Lewis was the first person to provide her husband with one thousand dollars a week guaranteed income, plus a car and driver.

John Beckman, himself, said that Jerry Lewis was very pleasant and courteous to work with. Ross Bellah, who was art director for Lewis' *The Ladies' Man* (1961) agreed, adding that although Lewis was a nut, he was especially kind to cast and crew, making sure they all got paid well for their time on the picture.

John Jr. remembers that from 1952 to 1961 his father typically would bring home a script, read it, break it down into scenes and come up with a preliminary budget. "Most of the talk was not about scripts but about the people he was working with. When Jane came along, it was the other way around, because her mother, Layne, had been a contract player and stand in for Bette Davis and Vivien Leigh."

In January 1967 Beckman underwent a minor operation. Layne said she felt that the studios were no longer interested in giving him work. He was sixty-nine, but quite young still and in pretty good health.

John Beckman now had a wife and daughter in addition to his son and was well beyond the age at which his son thought he would have to retire, or be fired. He thought it might be nice now to spend more time at his home in Cambria. He didn't know then that retirement was not to be in his future.

Television and Beyond

1962 was a difficult year for John Beckman. He suffered a heart attack and was forced to convalesce at Avila Beach. He and Layne had bought a home in Sherman Oaks with plans to remodel the garage and make it into a studio for John's painting, but then they rented a house north of there instead. After the heart attack, John and Layne found the house with room for a studio in Cambria which they bought, and it is this house which daughter Jane best remembers as her home.

Beckman had a blue-point Siamese cat named Sam here. Sam used to sit on top of the grandfather's clock. The Beckmans also had a weimeraner puppy named Cassandra and then a tiny Yorkshire terrier named Chrysanthemum, paying $500 for her. John Jr. said Chrissie was so excessively small that she could never be shown in dog shows. The Beckmans enjoyed telling the story about how they were seated once and said "Chrissie want uppy," and a lady nearby, looking on, thought they were crazy because she couldn't see any dog at all.

John Jr. said that in the period from 1963-1967 his father gave a one-man show of his paintings in a gallery on La Cienega Boulevard in Los Angeles. This was a period of prolific painting on Beckman's part. He used one end of a large living room for his studio, and the paintings he did demonstrated his versatility in style and approach.

But the gallery owner in Los Angeles believed that all the paintings by a painter should look alike. He wanted only paintings that identify the artist. This was awkward for Beckman because it suggested cranking out paintings in sausage-grinder style which was not his way. As a result, he sold only four paintings, which was a disappointment for him.

There was also a financial concern with the value of paintings. Beckman's close friend, Emil Kosa, had died, after building up a considerable reputation as a painter, leaving a legacy of paintings. The Internal Revenue Service appraised them at an unrealistic figure, making it difficult for Kosa's heirs.

John Jr. said his father lost interest in art showings after the La Cienega show. It is interesting that Beckman left John Jr. his paintings as part of his estate, with the Internal Revenue Service estimating their market value as $66,000.

After Mervyn LeRoy's death, John Beckman took a breather from movies and worked in television for the first time. He was art director for twenty-six episodes of *Profiles in Courage*, a television anthology based on John F. Kennedy's book. The program was shot in Culver City and produced by Robert Saudek, Gordon Oliver, and Michael Ritchie. Each episode was an hour long and centered around real figures in American history who had taken risks with their careers in the interest of a valuable, honest cause or principle. The programs aired on NBC from November 8, 1964 until May 9, 1965.

Then Beckman went back to movies again, until 1970 when he received an urgent call from his old friend, Ross Bellah, who said he was in a jam at Columbia television and couldn't get anyone to work for him. Beckman, now settled in with wife Layne, daughter Jane, and their antique shop in Cambria up in San Luis Obispo County, said he would only come if he were given billing as Assistant Art Director (perhaps to take some of the heat of responsibility off him) and if the hours were from 8:00 a.m. to 3:00 p.m. because Layne didn't want him away any longer. To Beckman's surprise, Bellah acceded to these requests, and a new career was born.

Television, the threat to motion pictures that everyone in movies hoped would go away, or fail, shares in common with movies the depiction of images on a screen, but the motion picture screen is twenty times larger than life, making people like Chaplin, Monroe, and De Niro into immense, giant gods and goddesses, while television reduces the image, making people look like tiny Lilliputians.

Consider the difference, for instance, in a Busby Berkeley movie musical where hundreds of women dance on an enormous set, and television—the June Taylor dancers on the Jackie Gleason Show, where only six dancers, at the most, are shown. Television is much more economical, tighter in its focus, ideal for zooming in on sports events like golf or football, or for showing two people engaged in conversation—Charlie Rose and a celebrity, for instance.

Art direction for television is generally much less demanding from a conceptual point of view. Sets are mostly realistic and tightly focused. The eyes of the audience are more easily deceived than are the eyes of a movie audience, where every little detail is blown up and magnified so much. Bellah, himself, said John Beckman probably designed most of his television sets with one hand tied behind his back.

This is not to say that the work of an art director isn't as grueling. It may even be more so in television, because you have to come up with a new idea every week. Ross Bellah tells about the early days at Columbia Studios:

> I did some of the first television shows that our studio did. As I remember, of course, it was black and white. They didn't have color yet. We didn't have much money and time to do our sets. I mean, I could do sets for little money because television couldn't afford much.
>
> For years, we did thirty-minute shows which they shot in three days. We'd have a production meeting on Friday, and we'd get the new script, read it, and then on Monday we'd have to design and build the sets.
>
> Sometimes we were doing two of those, with two sets of producers, scripts, and all. There were a lot of late nights. I've gone back to the studio at two or three o'clock in the

morning to see if the sets were going
to be ready in the morning.

John Beckman, Jr., said, "On *Designing Women,*
he'd be designing a set, not knowing what the story
line would be."

Ross Bellah, acknowledging the frantic pace of
television work, sums it up with, "Art directors have a
saying, 'We do those things you don't see behind the
people in front of the camera.'"

John Jr. said the *Designing Women* show would
shoot on Thursday. "On Friday, Dad would be working
on the next segment. Linda would be writing the next
script. It would be reviewed on Monday in New York.
There were times when the backers would want to
make revisions. Dad would have to guess what the
story line would be so that he would have a set for the
actors to work in on Tuesday. He never enjoyed a
television series more than this one. A lot was due to
the Thomasons; he enjoyed the people he worked
with."

John Beckman himself said, "I never worked so
hard in my life."

In line with this, a lot of effort goes into
producing a pilot that may or may not become a series.
Pilots are often audition pieces. If the audience and/or
executive bosses like it and respond, the show may go.
If they don't, it doesn't.

In the 1970s, John Beckman designed a number
of pilot shows. Some which didn't make it included
*Paracelsus, Mr. Deeds Goes to Town, The Girl with
Something Extra, Bob and Carol and Ted and Alice,
Lady Sheriff, Annie Hall,* and *Under the Yum Yum Tree.*

But some that succeeded were *Joe Forrester, Salvage II, Gibbsville,* and *Tabitha,* all done for Columbia.
For that studio, he also did twenty-six episodes of *The
Partridge Family* and, for his last four and a half years
of life he was art director for *Designing Women.*

John and Louise Beckman recalled that for the
Salvage series with Lloyd Bridges, nominally about a
junkyard, someone had the bright idea of bringing
down an iceberg from Alaska for one episode. The
producer, director, cameraman, and John as art
director flew up to Valdez where they chartered a bush

plane, flew under a glacier, landed, looked at it, and a chunk of ice came off. The pilot said he couldn't do it again. But Beckman and company had gotten their approach: A tugboat pulling the iceberg down the coast. It looked real, but it was actually a special effect.

Another time, Beckman designed a spaceship going to the moon. And for *Joe Forrester*, a detective show with William Conrad, Beckman designed a caged elevator that went up to a glassed-in greenhouse with orchid garden on a penthouse roof.

For Paramount, he did the pilot and series for *Nero Wolf, Ryan's Four, Liberty,* and did the series *Call to Glory*. He also worked three-months' each on *Cheers* and *Webster* for this studio.

It was good that he had these busy television assignments during this period because his wife Layne died tragically of a self-inflicted gunshot wound in February 1975, and, in 1981 he lost his sister, Johanna. The family believed that the heavy medication Layne was taking unbalanced her judgment.

There were some moments of happiness for Beckman, however. He had the pleasure of seeing his daughter Jane graduate from Cal Poly in San Luis Obispo and grandaughter Liz graduate from U.C.L.A. and enter the movie industry.

He sold his Sherman Oaks home in this period and rented the cottage on Ross Bellah's property in Studio City.

He had been quite devastated by Layne's death, and kept the home in Cambria almost exactly the way it was, as a shrine to Layne. Daughter Jane inherited the home after her father's death.

Another major occupation for John Beckman during the 1960s and 1970s especially, although it was, in a real sense, his life's work, was his painting.

Cambria is a rarified community where many artists live, and Beckman often painted landscapes in oil—seascapes, mountains—bold, imaginative, semi-abstract, colorful canvases during this period.

In 1995-1996, a retrospective exhibition of his paintings took place at The Sovereign Collection at the Oregon History Center in Portland, Oregon, under the direction of Robert L. Joki, from November 1995 through the middle of February 1996.

In 1979, he and Ross Bellah were co-art directors for a two-hour Green/Epstein television production, *Breaking Up Is Hard to Do*, for Columbia Pictures Television. Lou Antonio was the director, Gaynbe Rescher the photographer, and the cast included Ted Bessell and Jeff Conaway.

In that year also, John got a bad case of influenza and became dehydrated. His grandaughter Liz was in college at U.C.L.A. At the end of 1978 and into 1979 she was living with him in his Sherman Oaks home. He also paid for her apartment in Westwood Village. She came home and found him fibrillating, called an ambulance, and he was hospitalized for two weeks.

He had been working at Paramount at the time, but nobody called Paramount to inform them what had happened. Still, John recovered and lived and worked for another ten years after that setback.

In 1980, Bellah and Beckman again teamed up to be art directors for the same producers and studio in another made-for-television movie called *To Find a Son*. Delbert Mann directed, Gerald Perry Finnerman was the photographer, and the cast included Richard Thomas and Justin Dana.

For Columbia, Beckman also was art director for a two-hour movie called *The Dream Merchants*, and, with Ross Bellah he was co-art director on *Kate's Secret*, another two-hour movie, produced at Columbia, which aired on NBC November 11, 1986. This show starred Meredith Baxter Birney as a beautiful woman and an ideal wife, suffering from the disease of the month—in this case, bulimia. Arthur Allan Seidelman directed, and the photographer was Dennis Dalzell.

Also in 1986, John Beckman was signed as art director on a prestigious two-hour movie version of the *Boy's Town* story, this time called *Miracle of the Heart: A Boystown Story*. For this, he went on location in Boy's Town and Omaha, Nebraska. The show starred Art Carney as the priest and Casey Siemaszko as the thieving juvenile dumped at Boy's Town against his will. Georg Stanford Brown was director, and the photographer was James Pergola.

Harry Thomason, producer of *Designing Women*, along with his wife Linda Bloodworth Thomason, loves to tell the story about how he first met John Beckman.

In 1978, Thomason was new to the business and California, so when Ross Bellah called, suggesting John Beckman for the job of art director on a movie Thomason was about to make in Phoenix, Bellah said, "But you probably won't want him. He's eighty years old."

Thomason says he remembered the words of his old high school coach who said, "Never go into battle unless you have some people who have been there before." And so, he hired John, loved him, and took him out to Phoenix where they made the movie.

Then, in 1986, when he was doing the pilot for *Designing Women* and in the market for an art director, Bellah called again, saying, "Listen, I've got this person. I really like him, but he's eighty-eight years old."

"You talking about John Beckman?" asked Thomason.

Bellah admitted he was.

"Get him over here," replied Thomason. "He's got the job."

The set design for *Designing Women* was always pretty much a constant—the living room of the Sugarbakers' home in Atlanta, Georgia, from which Julia and Suzanne Sugarbaker (played by Dixie Carter and Delta Burke), plus their friends and co-workers, Jean Smart, Annie Potts, and Meshach Taylor, ran an interior decorating business. Occasionally, one of the other rooms would be shown, and, once in a while, another location, like a church, but the set remained essentially the same all the years Beckman was there, a cheerful background for a realistic situation comedy.

This was a far cry from Beckman's first year in the movies where he worked on *Nana, Benvenuto Cellini, The House of Rothschild, The Return of Bulldog Drummond, One Night of Love*, and *Kid Millions*. Yet John Beckman brought the same degree of professionalism and artistic integrity to *Designing Women* that he did to all his projects. And he did it at ninety-one.

He was very proud of his church set for *Designing Women* in 1987, although they didn't get around to shooting it until two in the morning. Beckman was always up to the mark. His son concurred: "If it's something you enjoy doing, working hard is not the kind of stress that worries one."

Linda Bloodworth Thomason, Harry's wife, who conceived *Designing Women* and wrote many of its episodes, found John Beckman enchanting. She loved hearing his life story with all its lore about the Czar of Russia. She confided that she would have dated him if she were younger and available. She told her husband that *My Dinner With André* was a B-movie compared to dinner with John. She felt that dinners with John were world history lessons and a philosophy lesson on how the world should be.

Nearing the end of his life, John Beckman was still contributing his imagination and time to the art world. He was as much admired now as he had been when he was a young man. He set standards for honest, hard, creative work, and for courteous conduct in the industry, and he did his business with few complaints.

He had had a rich, dramatic personal and professional life, the devotion of his two wives, his children, two granddaughters, and his many friends. One night, October 25, 1989, he simply closed his eyes, fell asleep, and never woke again.

His life and career practically spanned the entire twentieth century.

At the funeral services for John Beckman, Chuck Liddell told how Beckman had stayed away from Catalina Island so long because he had heard a false rumor that his murals had been whitewashed over. Liddell said Beckman couldn't make the fiftieth anniversary because he was sick, but he did make the sixtieth and was the life of the party, receiving a standing ovation from the audience and dancing with many women at the celebration. He also joined a few of the tour groups, adding commentary of his own, impressing everybody, and signing autographs for young and old alike.

Harry Thomason remembered how, at the end of the work week, everyone on *Designing Women* would hobble home to rest on the week ends because of the pressure of work, while John, on the following Monday mornings, would be chipper as usual, saying, "Oh, I flew to Philadelphia and had dinner. Then I went to Hawaii for the week end, and I had a marvelous time." Thomason said the *Designing Women* staff all had a marvelous time with John, too.

Harry Thomason's final words were that John Beckman "was better dressed, better spoken, better traveled, better mannered, and that modesty, those good manners were what kept him from admitting he was better than others. Gable, Chaplin, Garbo, Valentino, Bogart, Aimee Semple McPherson—the list goes on and on—they were his contemporaries. All these people were stars, but John was a star, too. A star of life. They were all better off for having known him."

For John Gabriel Beckman, the applause may have been silent, but it was always there.

Appendix A

1934 NANA, Dorothy Arzner, director; Richard Day, art director; Gregg Toland photographer; cast, Anna Sten; Goldwyn/United Artists.

1934 HOUSE OF ROTHSCHILD, Alfred Weiler, director; Richard Day, art director; J. Peverell Marley, photographer; cast, George Arliss, Loretta Young; Twentieth Century.

1934 BULLDOG DRUMMOND STRIKES BACK, Roy Del Ruth, director; Richard Day, art director; J. Peverell Marley, photographer; cast, Ronald Colman, Loretta Young, C. Aubrey Smith; United Artists.

1934 THE AFFAIRS OF CELLINI, Gregory La Cava, director; Richard Day, art director; Charles Rosher, photographer; cast, Constance Bennett, Fredric March; Twentieth Century Fox/United Artists.

1934 KID MILLIONS, Roy del Ruth, director; Richard Day, art director; Ray June, photographer; cast, Eddie Cantor, Ethel Merman, Ann Sothern; Goldwyn/United Artists.

1934 ONE NIGHT OF LOVE, Victor Schertzinger, director; Stephen Goosson, art director; Joseph Walker, photographer; cast, Grace Moore, Tullio Carminati, Lyle Talbot; Columbia.

1935 CARDINAL RICHELIEU, Roland V. Lee, director; Richard Day, art director; J. Peverell Marley, photographer; cast, George Arliss, Maureen O'Sullivan; Twentieth Century-Fox/United Artists.

1935 CLIVE OF INDIA, Richard Boleslavski, director; Richard Day, art director; J. Peverell Marley, photographer; cast, Ronald Colman, Loretta Young; Twentieth Century/United Artists.

1935 LES MISERABLES, Richard Boleslavski, director; Richard Day, art director; Gregg Toland, photographer; cast, Fredric March, Charles Laughton; Twentieth Century.

1935 FOLIES BERGERES DE PARIS, Roy del Ruth, director; Richard Day, Alexander Golitzen, art directors; Barney McGill and J. Peverell Marley, photographers; cast, Maurice Chevalier, Ann Sothern, Merle Oberon; Twentieth Century-Fox/ United Artists.

1935 A MIDSUMMER NIGHT'S DREAM, Max Reinhardt, William Dieterle, directors; Anton Grot, art director; Hal Mohr, photographer; cast, James Cagney, Mickey Rooney, Olivia de Havilland; Warner Brothers.

1936 LLOYDS OF LONDON, Henry King, director; William Darling, art director; Bert Glennon, photographer; cast, Freddie Bartholomew, Tyrone Power, Madeleine Carroll; Twentieth Century-Fox.

1936 MR. DEEDS GOES TO TOWN, Frank Capra, director; Stephen Goosson, art director; Joseph Walker, photographer; cast, Gary Cooper, Jean Arthur; Columbia.

1936 THE PETRIFIED FOREST, Archie L. Mayo, director; John Hughes, art director; Sol Polito, photographer; cast, Bette Davis, Humphrey Bogart, Leslie Howard; Warner Brothers.

1937 LOST HORIZON, Frank Capra, director; Stephen Goosson, art director; Joseph Walker, photographer; cast, Ronald Colman, Jane Wyatt, John Howard, (Academy Award winner, Best Interior Decoration): Columbia.

1937 THE PRINCE AND THE PAUPER, William Keighley, director; Robert Haas, art director; Sol Polito, photographer; cast, Errol Flynn, Claude Rains; Warner Brothers.

1937 THE LIFE OF EMILE ZOLA, William Dieterle, director; Anton Grot, art director; Tony Gaudio, photographer; cast, Paul Muni, Joseph Schildkraut; Warner Brothers.

1938 THE ADVENTURES OF ROBIN HOOD, William Keighley and Michael Curtiz, directors; Carl Jules Weyl, art director; Tony Gaudio, Sol Polito, W. Howard Greene, photographers; cast, Errol Flynn, Olivia de Havilland; (Academy Award winner, Best Interior Decoration); Warner Brothers.

1938 FOOLS FOR SCANDAL, Mervyn LeRoy, director; Anton Grot, art director; Ted Tetzlaff, photographer; cast, Carole Lombard, Fernand Gravet, Ralph Bellamy; Warner Brothers.

1939 JUAREZ, William Dieterle, director; Anton Grot, art director; Tony Gaudio, photographer; cast, Bette Davis, Paul Muni, John Garfield; Warner Brothers.

1939 THE RAINS CAME, Clarence Brown, director; William Darling and George Dudley, art directors; Arthur Miller, photographer; cast, Tyrone Power, Myrna Loy, George Brent; (Academy Award nomination, Best Art Direction): Twentieth Century-Fox.

1939 THE ROARING TWENTIES, Raoul Walsh, director; Max Parker, art director; Ernest Haller, photographer; cast, Humphrey Bogart, James Cagney, Priscilla Lane; Warner Brothers.

1940 A DISPATCH FROM REUTERS, William Dieterle, director; Anton Grot, art
      director; James Wong Howe, photographer; cast, Edward G. Robinson, Edna
      Best, Eddie Albert; Warner Brothers.

1941 HIGH SIERRA, Raoul Walsh, director; Ted Smith, art director; Tony Gaudio,
      photographer; cast, Humphrey Bogart, Ida Lupino; Warner Brothers.

1941 THE MALTESE FALCON, John Huston, director; Robert Haas, art director; Arthur
      Edeson, photographer; cast, Humphrey Bogart, Mary Astor, Sydney Greenstreet;
      Warner Brothers.

1942 CASABLANCA, Michael Curtiz, director; Carl Jules Weyl, art director; Arthur
      Edeson, photographer; cast, Humphrey Bogart, Ingrid Bergman, Paul Henreid;
      Warner Brothers.

1942 THE HARD WAY, Vincent Sherman, director; Max Parker, art director; James
      Wong Howe, photographer; cast, Ida Lupino, Dennis Morgan, Joan Leslie,
      Jack Carson; Warner Brothers.

1942 THIS IS THE ARMY, Michael Curtiz, director; John Hughes and John Koenig, art
      directors; Bert Glennon, Sol Polito, photographers; cast, George Murphy, Ronald
      Reagan, Joan Leslie; Warner Brothers.

1942 ACROSS THE PACIFIC, John Huston, director: Robert Haas, Hugh Reticker, art
      directors; Arthur Edeson, photographer: cast, Humphrey Bogart, Mary Astor;
      Warner Brothers.

1943 PRINCESS O'ROURKE, Norman Krasna, director; Max Parker, art director; Ernest
      Haller, photographer; cast, Olivia de Havilland, Robert Cummings, Jane Wyman;
      Warner Brothers.

1944 ARSENIC AND OLD LACE, Frank Capra, director; Max Parker, art director; Sol
      Polito, photographer; cast, Cary Grant, Priscilla Lane, Josephine Hull; Warner
      Brothers.

1944 MR. SKEFFINGTON, Vincent Sherman, director; Robert Haas, art director; Ernest
      Haller, photographer; cast, Bette Davis, Claude Rains; Warner Brothers.

1945 MILDRED PIERCE, Michael Curtiz, director; Anton Grot, art director; Ernest
      Haller, photographer; cast, Joan Crawford, Zachary Scott, Ann Blyth; Warner
      Brothers.

1945 RHAPSODY IN BLUE, Irving Rapper, director; Anton Grot and John Hughes, art
      directors; Sol Polito, Merritt Gerstad, photographers; cast, Robert Alda, Alexis
      Smith, Oscar Levant; Warner Brothers.

1947 THE TWO MRS. CARROLLS, Peter Godfrey, director; Anton Grot, art director; J. Peverell Marley, photographer; cast, Barbara Stanwyck, Humphrey Bogart, Alexis Smith; Warner Brothers.

1948 JOHNNY BELINDA, Jean Negulesco, director; Robert Haas, art director; Ted McCord, photographer; cast, Jane Wyman, Lew Ayres, Agnes Moorhead; (Academy Award nomination, Best Black and White Art Direction): Warner Brothers.

1948 ROMANCE ON THE HIGH SEAS, Michael Curtiz, director; Anton Grot, art director; Howard Winterbottom, set decorator; Elwood Bredell, photographer; cast, Doris Day, Jack Carson, Oscar Levant, Janis Paige; Warner Brothers.

1950 THE GLASS MENAGERIE, Irving Rapper, director; Robert Haas, art director; Robert Burks, photographer; cast, Gertrude Lawrence, Kirk Douglas, Jane Wyman, Arthur Kennedy; Warner Brothers.

JOHN GABRIEL BECKMAN
AS ART DIRECTOR

1947 MONSIEUR VERDOUX, Charlie Chaplin, director; John Beckman, art director; Rollie Totheroe, photographer; cast, Charlie Chaplin, Martha Raye; United Artists.

1948 THE DECISION OF CHRISTOPHER BLAKE, Peter Godfrey, director; John Beckman, art director; Karl Freund, photographer; cast, Alexis Smith, Robert Douglas, Cecil Kellaway; Warner Brothers.

1952 THE IRON MISTRESS, Gordon Douglas, director; John Beckman, art director; John Seitz, photographer; cast, Alan Ladd, Virginia Mayo, Warner Brothers.

1952 SPRINGFIELD RIFLE, Andre de Toth, director; John Beckman, art director; Edwin Du Par, photographer; cast, Gary Cooper, Phyllis Thaxter, David Brian; Warner Brothers.

1953 THE SYSTEM, Lewis Seiler, director; John Beckman, art director; Edwin DuPar, photographer; cast, Frank Lovejoy, Joan Weldon, Bob Arthur; Warner Brothers.

1953 BY THE LIGHT OF THE SILVERY MOON, David Butler, director; John Beckman, art director; Wilfrid M. Cline, photographer; cast, Doris Day, Gordon MacRae; Warner Brothers.

1953 CALAMITY JANE, David Butler, director: John Beckman, art director; Wilfrid M. Cline, photographer; cast, Doris Day, Howard Keel: Warner Brothers.

1954 THE YOUNG AT HEART, Gordon Douglas, director; John Beckman, art director; Ted McCord, photographer; cast, Frank Sinatra, Doris Day, Ethel Barrymore; Warner Brothers.

1955 BATTLE CRY, Raoul Walsh, director; John Beckman, art director; Sid Hickox, photographer; cast, Van Heflin, Aldo Ray, Dorothy Malone; Warner Brothers.

1956 HELL ON FRISCO BAY, Frank Tuttle, director; John Beckman, art director; John Seitz, photographer; cast, Alan Ladd, Edward G. Robinson, Joanne Dru; Jaguar/Warner Brothers.

1956 THE BAD SEED, Mervyn LeRoy, director; John Beckman, art director; Hal Rosson, photographer; cast, Nancy Kelly, Patty McCormack, Eileen Heckart; Warner Brothers.

1956 TOWARD THE UNKNOWN, Mervyn LeRoy, director; John Beckman, art director; Hal Rosson, photographer; cast, William Holden, Lloyd Nolan, Virginia Leith; Toluca/Warner Brothers.

1958 HOME BEFORE DARK, Mervyn LeRoy, director; John Beckman, art director; Joseph Biroc, photographer; cast, Jean Simmons, Dan O'Herlihy, Rhonda Fleming; Warner Brothers.

1958 LAFAYETTE ESCADRILLE, William Wellman, director; John Beckman, art director; William Clothier, photographer; cast, Tab Hunter, Clint Eastwood; Warner Brothers.

1959 THE HELEN MORGAN STORY, Michael Curtiz, director; John Beckman, art director; Ted McCord, photographer; cast, Ann Blyth, Paul Newman, Richard Carlson; Warner Brothers.

1959 THE F.B.I. STORY, Mervyn LeRoy, director; John Beckman, art director; Joseph Biroc, photographer; cast, James Stewart, Vera Miles; Warner Brothers.

1960 WAKE ME WHEN IT'S OVER, Mervyn LeRoy, director; Lyle Wheeler, John Beckman, art directors; Leon Shamroy, photographer; cast, Ernie Kovacs, Don Knotts, Dick Shawn; Fox.

1961 A MAJORITY OF ONE, Mervyn LeRoy, director; John Beckman, art director; Harry Stradling, Sr., photographer; cast, Alec Guinness, Rosalind Russell; Warner Brothers.

1961 THE DEVIL AT FOUR O'CLOCK, Mervyn LeRoy, director; John Beckman, art director; Joseph Biroc, photographer; cast, Spencer Tracy, Frank Sinatra; Columbia.

1962 GYPSY, Mervyn LeRoy, director; John Beckman, art director; Harry Stradling Sr., photographer; cast, Rosalind Russell, Natalie Wood, Karl Malden; Warner Brothers.

1963 MARY, MARY, Mervyn LeRoy, director; John Beckman, art director; Ralph S. Hurst, set decorator; Harry Stradling, photographer; cast, Debbie Reynolds, Barry Nelson, Michael Rennie; Warner Brothers.

1966 THE TROUBLE WITH ANGELS, Ida Lupino, director; John Beckman, art director; Lionel Linden, photographer; cast, Rosalind Russell, Hayley Mills, Binnie Barnes, Gypsy Rose Lee; Columbia.

1967 WHO'S MINDING THE MINT?, Howard Morris, director; John Beckman, art director; Joseph Biroc, photographer; cast, Milton Berle, Joey Bishop, Jack Gilford, Walter Brennan; Columbia.

1968 ASSIGNMENT TO KILL, Sheldon Reynolds, director; John Beckman, art director; Harold Lipstein, Enzo Barboni, photographers; cast, John Gielgud, Patrick O'Neal, Joan Hackett, Oscar Homolka; Warner Brothers-Seven Arts.

1968 IN ENEMY COUNTRY, Harry Keller, director; Alexander Golitzen, John Beckman, art directors; Loyal Griggs, photographer; cast, Tony Franciosa, Anjanette Comer, Guy Stockwell; Universal,

1969 HOOK, LINE, AND SINKER, George Marshall, director; John Beckman, art director; Frank Tuttle, set decorator; W. Wallace Kelley, photographer; cast, Jerry Lewis, Peter Lawford, Anne Francis; Columbia.

1970 WHICH WAY TO THE FRONT?, Jerry Lewis, director; John Beckman, art director; W. Wallace Kelley, photographer; cast, Jerry Lewis, Jan Murray, Kaye Ballard; Warner Brothers.

JOHN GABRIEL BECKMAN

Art Director

TELEVISION CREDITS

1972-1989

PROFILES IN COURAGE (book by President John F. Kennedy)
26 episodes for Robert Saudek at Culver City

COLUMBIA TELEVISION

MR. DEEDS GOES TO TOWN	pilot
PARACELSIS	pilot
GIRL WITH SOMETHING EXTRA	pilot
BOB, CAROL, TED AND ALICE	pilot
LADY SHERIFF	pilot
ANNIE HALL	pilot
UNDER THE YUM, YUM TREE	pilot
JOE FORRESTER	pilot/series
SALVAGE II	pilot/series
GIBBSVILLE	pilot/series
TABITHA	series
THE PARTRIDGE FAMILY	series
THE DREAM MERCHANTS	Movie of the Week
KATE'S SECRET	Movie of the Week
MIRACLE OF THE HEART: A BOYSTOWN STORY	Movie of the Week
DESIGNING WOMEN	pilot/Series

PARAMOUNT PICTURES

NERO WOLF	pilot/series
RYAN'S FOUR	pilot/series
CALL TO GLORY	series
LIBERTY	pilot/series
CHEERS	series (3 months)
WEBSTER	series (3 months)

Appendix B Photographs

John Gabriel Beckman c. 1922
Photo: Collection Louise & John Beckman, Jr.

Exterior murals by John Gabriel Beckman.
Bottom: The Casino, Catalina Island.

John Gabriel Beckman's exterior murals
for Catalina Island's Casino. Lower right, red-haired
mermaid, the only mural set in tile.

Beckman's exterior murals. The Casino,
Catalina Island.

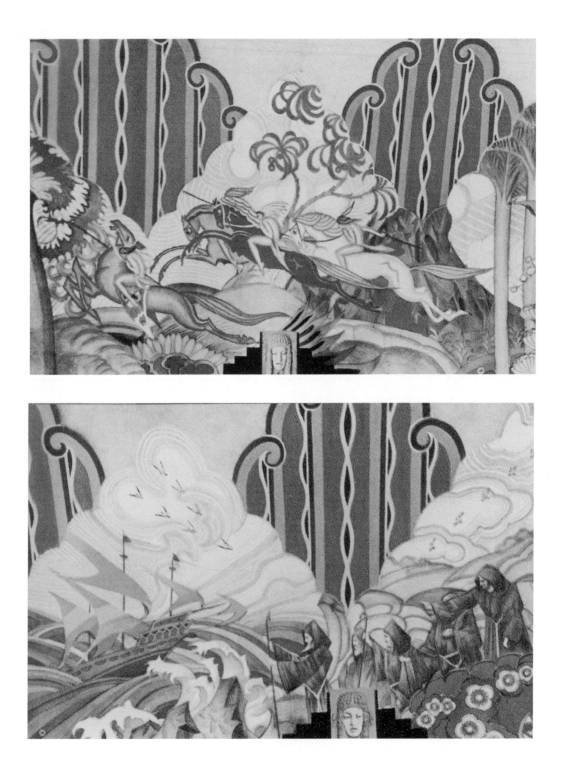

Top, design showing Native Americans on horses; Bottom, Spanish ship with
friars, murals by John Gabriel Beckman for interior of Avalon Theatre, Catalina.

John Gabriel Beckman's murals for
The Chinese Theatre, Hollywood.

John Gabriel Beckman's murals for
The Chinese Theatre, Hollywood.

John Gabriel Beckman's murals for
The Chinese Theatre, Hollywood.

Jean Simmons in *Home Before Dark*, Mervyn LeRoy, Director; John Beckman, Art Director. Photo from Warner Brothers.

Natalie Wood in *Gypsy*, Mervyn LeRoy, Director; John Beckman,, Art Director. Photo from Warner Brothers.

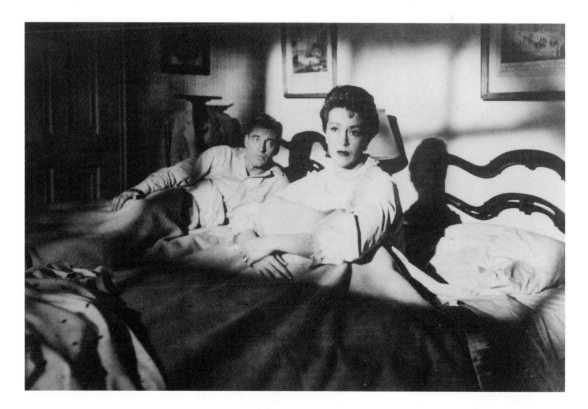

William Hopper and Nancy Kelly in *The Bad Seed*, Mervyn LeRoy, Director; John Beckman, Art Director. Photo from Warner Brothers.

Charlie Chaplin, Martha Raye in *Monsieur Verdoux*, Charles Chaplin, Director; John Beckman, Art Director. Photo from United Artists.

Margaret Hoffman, Marilyn Nash, Charlie Chaplin in *Monsieur Verdoux,* Charles Chaplin, Director; John Beckman, Art Director. Photo from United Artists.

Shangri-La set for *Lost Horizon*. Frank Capra, Director; Stephen Goosson, Art Director. Photo from Columbia Pictures.

Ronald Colman and H. B. Warner in *Lost Horizon*. Frank Capra, Director; Stephen Goosson, Art Director. Photo from Columbia Pictures.

Gordon MacRae and Doris Day in *By the Light of the Silvery Moon*. David Butler, Director; John Beckman, Art Director. Photo from Warner Brothers.

Jan Murray, Steve Franken, John Wood, Dack Rambo, and Jerry Lewis in *Which Way to the Front?* Jerry Lewis, Director; John Beckman, Art Director. Photo from Warner Brothers.

Delta Burke, Annie Potts, Dixie Carter, and Jean Smart in *Designing Women*.
Art Director, John Beckman. *Designing Women* photo © 2003 Sony Pictures Television

John Gabriel Beckman
Photo: Collection Louise & John Beckman, Jr.

NOTES

CHAPTER 1: SOINTULA

This chapter relies heavily on John Gabriel Beckman's own return to Sointula in July 1987 and his son's and Louise Beckman's reminiscences of the same area. A videotape was made of Beckman's return visit at that time and a copy was given to me for use in this book. I also had access to a Beckman History tape made by John G. Beckman, Jr., in November 1998 and "Family Notes with Jane," by John and Jane Beckman written in November 1999. In addition, my own travels in the Puget Sound, Seattle, and British Columbia area, plus additional reading, helped me understand better the geography, meteorology, and native inhabitants of the region.

CHAPTER 2: APPRENTICE TO THE WORLD

Page 17: The Beckmans all had great interest in automobiles. When I first met them in 1945, they had six cars in their yard in North Hollywood: a 1933 Marmon 16, a 1914 Locomobile, a 1937 Packard 12-cylinder limousine, a 1933 Lincoln town car, a 1926 Franklin, and a 1926 Stutz. For more information about my first encounters with the Beckmans and their automobiles, here is a copy of "Hunting Beckmans," one of the two talks I presented in the Avalon Theater in Catalina on the subject of John Gabriel Beckman, this one to the International Art Deco Congress on May 20, 1997, (the other speech was to the Society of Architectural Historians, Southern California Chapter, on March 23, 1996):

HUNTING BECKMANS

I first met John Gabriel Beckman in 1945 when I was in the U.S. Navy. His son, John Jr., was stationed with me at the Seal Beach Naval Ammunition and Net Depot in California and invited me to spend the night at his parents' home on Tujunga Avenue in North Hollywood. My first impression of his father was that he was a tall, elegantly slim, reserved and courtly man. I thought he dressed very smartly and was quietly supportive of both his wife and son. John's mother was a warm, also quiet woman, with understanding brown eyes and brunette hair. She originally came from Farmington, Iowa, and had met Mr. Beckman on a Sierra Club outing when she mistook him for another man she knew. He answered her welcoming hand-wave, and they found they were very compatible and married eventually.

Their home on Tujunga Avenue, as I remember it, was a comfortable unpretent-
ious white California bungalow type home with a large yard filled with the
Beckmans' six cars: a 1914 Locomobile, a 1933 Marmon 16, a 1933 Lincoln formal
sedan, a 1926 Franklin, a 1926 Stutz and a 1937 Packard 12-cylinder limousine. Both
men were avid automobile aficionados and knew a great deal about all makes of
cars.

I knew Mr. Beckman was an art director for films, but there was no indication of
this in the man at home, or in the home itself for that matter. I remember the living
room was filled with antiques, including a Steinway rosewood square grand piano,
and that the family tiptoed around the borders of the room so as not to disturb its
valuable contents. In the library they had a Weber upright player piano, an Edison
cylinder phonograph with morning glory horn, and a grandfather clock, now
gracing John Jr. and Louise Beckman's home in Vancouver, Washington. Obviously,
these were prized possessions and they were highly respectful of them. So was I.

John Jr. talked more about film personalities than did the father. John Jr. knew
the actress Wanda Hendrix, among others, and played some recordings he and she
had made together. John's mother, Nellie, always read the ads on antiques in
newspapers. Often somebody would move from an outside state to California after
their daughter had been signed by a studio. Nellie met Wanda Hendrix and her
mother through the antique sales. Wanda's mother had run a restaurant in
Jacksonville, Florida. Wanda had played Snow White in a high school play and a
talent scout had seen her and brought her to Hollywood. Nellie wanted John Jr. to
meet this beautiful girl. John Jr. at first protested, saying, "I can meet my own girls,"
but his mother persisted and John and Wanda became friends.

Wanda Hendrix shone brightly in a few films, married the great war hero Audie
Murphy, who very creditably played the lead in John Huston's film *The Red Badge of
Courage,* but then divorced him in 1952. John Jr. saw a different Wanda after that.
She asked him about the possibility of working at Warner Brothers. But when John
Jr. mentioned a certain casting director, Wanda replied, "He doesn't hire any women
who won't sleep with him." John Jr. felt her life hadn't turned out the way she had
hoped it would.

On another occasion, when John Jr. and I were heading back to our base, he
said he wanted to stop by the Charlie Chaplin studios where his father was working
as art director for Chaplin's film *Monsieur Verdoux.* He asked if I wanted to go on the
set with him and meet Chaplin, but I, impatient for some reason or another, declined,
and have regretted this ever since. Both John Jr. and I, of course, were sailors in
uniform during World War II, and John Jr. reported that when he entered he walked
across the sound stage. "All of Chaplin's assistants were lined up with their backs
toward me. Chaplin was giving notes to them. He spotted me, dressed in my Navy
uniform. I walked over. My Dad introduced me. He was very cordial."

I remember noting how agreeable the Beckman family was, considering how
the father's occupation was centered around film, but perhaps that was just because
it ran counter to the conventional stereotypical view of what anybody involved with
Hollywood's life was like. I admired the Beckman family immensely; they appeared
to be genuinely nice, intelligent, creative people without any traces of guile or
jealousy in their makeups.

Among the interesting by-products of my relationship with the Beckmans was
the magnificent car Robinson Smith and I purchased during our Navy days. We were
looking for a car to share on liberties in Los Angeles and John Jr., after showing us
his Stutz, took us to Figueroa Street where we came upon a 1930 Cadillac 16-cylinder
black sedan which we all admired. We had not walked fifty feet farther when John
spotted the blond custom-made 1931 16-cylinder Cadillac that Howard Hughes had
given as a token of his affection to Jean Harlow. After Harlow's death in 1936, the car
had sat in storage until it was released to the Carlin Car Company on Figueroa Street.
John Jr. crawled under the car, examining the bore and stroke, looked at the engine,
the interior, the exterior, and persuaded us to buy this beauty. We paid $795 for it
and owned it until we were discharged from the Navy in the summer of 1946. Then,
after Rob and I flew home back East, the Beckmans took our car and sold it to a
collector who lived in Santa Maria. Naturally, a car like that, of which only fourteen
were made, is worth well over a quarter of a million dollars today.

In the fall of 1946, John Jr. enrolled in the Yale School of Architecture and came East where he visited Rob Smith's family in New Hampshire and mine on Long Island and he settled in to his studies at Yale. He was a great favorite in my family. Since I was at Bowdoin College in Maine, John also came up there to visit me and I went down to New Haven where he introduced me to several members of the Yale School of Drama, including one, Nikos Psacharopoulos, who was to be a future teacher of mine when I entered the School of Drama in 1956. I remember that John Jr. lived in the Winchester Hospital in West Haven, where some returning veterans were housed. He had stationery printed up, reading:

John G. Beckman, Jr.
Yale School of Architecture
210-A, East Ward Wing
Winchester Veterans' Hospital
West Haven, Connecticut

I remember John's room. He had two female canaries he had bought at the ten cent store, lots of creative clutter in paper, books, and sketch pads, and, of course, his unfailing cheerful manner and appreciative smile. John was always polite and well-mannered, attributes shared by his father. Originally, John had had a roommate, but the roomie didn't like canaries, and so moved. John also had an RCA Victor 1929 phono-radio combination-transistor electric and hand-cranked. The head was acoustical or electric and the turntable was electric.

John Jr. spent one year at Yale and then transferred back to California. In December of 1951, we had some sad news from him. His mother had developed cancer and then apparently died of a heart attack. We sent flowers in memory of this lovely woman. She is buried in the Hollywood Hills Forest Lawn Cemetery.

In 1952 I married Verna Rudd Trimble of Montclair, New Jersey, and asked John Jr. if he would be an usher at our wedding in St. Luke's Episcopal Church. His answer was yes, saying that he and his father would be flying in on Saturday, April 5th for the wedding and would return the next day to Los Angeles. They stayed at my family's home on Long Island, and my father met them at Laguardia Airport in New York. Both Rudd and I couldn't believe the kindness of father and son—to fly all that way for our wedding. It has always been one of our most cherished memories of that day.

The scene now shifts to 1956 because Rudd and I left the United States in March of 1953 and spent the next two years living and working in Switzerland. Upon our return, I taught for a year at Northeastern University in Boston, finished up a Master's degree at Harvard University, and then entered the Yale School of Drama in 1956 as a candidate for the Doctor of Fine Arts degree in Drama. I thought of John Jr. when we arrived in New Haven, and we contacted him in California, but then lost touch with him until we received a notice that he had married. By that time, his father had remarried and moved to Sherman Oaks, and apparently had an unlisted number, so I sat back, confident that John would call us eventually and that we would resume our friendship. His life must have been changing as ours was, too.

The lost years in our friendship are those between 1956 and 1985. I had only vague clues—John Jr. was working for an architectural firm on Geary Street in San Francisco, then he moved to Novato. His father had become a major art director at Warner Brothers. I knew this from television credits. But that was all.

In 1983, my wife and I moved to San Luis Obispo, where I was Head of the Theatre and Dance Department at Cal Poly. Then in 1985, our daughter Brooke, a recent graduate of Sarah Lawrence College, took a job as costume assistant on a stage production of *Bogart* at the Pan Andreas Theatre in Hollywood. On this show, she worked with the costumer, Camille Abbott, and a young man named Chris Senter.

She asked them if they had ever heard of John Gabriel Beckman, and both said, yes, they had indeed. Camille had worked with Mr. Beckman whom she looked up to with the greatest respect, and Chris' father, Jack Senter, had also worked with him. Through the Senters, Brooke got John Sr.'s, telephone number in Cambria, where he was now living, and I gave him a call:

"Mr. Beckman? This is Roger Kenvin. Do you remember me?"

"I certainly do. I was at your wedding."

That was the beginning of the reconciliation, and soon, both father and son, and John's second wife, Louise, were in our living room in San Luis Obispo, and the years were melting away, bringing us all back to our friendship again, this time with the addition of the wonderful Louise, about whom John Senior rhapsodized.

On two occasions in 1986 and 1987, Rudd and I had two visits with John Senior and went to dinner with him at his favorite restaurant, the Wine Bistro on Ventura Boulevard in Studio City. He was living in Ross Bellah's cottage set in Bellah's beautiful Japanese garden home on Bellingham Avenue in Studio City, a home that John Sr. occupied for nine years until his death in 1989. One night, John Sr. showed us some of his art work and also gave us souvenir programs and press releases from the studios which he had received prior to the Motion Picture Academy ceremonies.

The first night at dinner, John Sr. paid the bill. Everybody at Wine Bistro treated him like a god. The restaurant is favored by people in the industry who work in television and at the studios nearby. On this night, Katherine Helmond and her husband were there, and I recognized Timothy Busfield from *Thirty-Something* at the little round table just inside the door. I asked Mr. Beckman a lot of questions about his life and the industry that night. As always, I was impressed by the energy, verve, and style of this man, still working, now as art director for Harry and Linda Bloodworth Thomason on *Designing Women*. Mr. Beckman arranged for Rudd, Brooke, and me to attend a taping of *Designing Women*.

When we arrived at the Warner Brothers' studio in Burbank, we were given the VIP treatment. After all, the revered John Gabriel Beckman had made the arrangments himself. We were able to drive our car right onto the lot, ushered into prime seats in the reserved forward section and made to feel very special indeed. We enjoyed the taping, including the fluffs with the delightful Alice Ghostley losing her cool twice, and seeing Dixie Carter, Jean Smart, Delta Burke, Meshach Taylor, and Annie Potts go through their paces. Plus we were able to talk with grips, cameramen, and even the director, who, for this episode was the great child star, Jackie Cooper. The taping went on until very late, but we stayed for every minute of it.

At our second dinner, I paid the bill and we brought along our daughter's roommate, a young woman whom I had directed in shows back in Virginia. She was, of course, quite taken with Mr. Beckman, and he trotted out some of his best stories to tell. I remember he spoke very highly of Errol Flynn, and said that Flynn, after completion of his pictures, would often throw parties at the Sportsmen's Lodge. He also told me that Jack Warner and he always had a good relationship, that Warner always gave him what he wanted in the way of money for sets or decoration. What he failed to relay, I think, is that his natural courteousness inspired courteousness in others. It would be hard to imagine anyone ever being uncivil to Mr. Beckman.

In 1987, Rudd and I made a trip north by train to Washington, British Columbia, and Oregon, and stopped in Portland, where we visited John and Louise in their Vancouver, Washington, home and went on a fascinating boat trip with them on the Columbia River. I often think of how proud John's grandfather would have been knowing that John Jr. has worked for architects, the profession Dr. Oswald Beckman had wanted his son to follow. And John Gabriel Beckman, I know, was proud of his grandaughter Liz who produces promotional films for backers to see at film festivals. Both John Jr. and his daughter Liz continue the Beckman tradition of architecture and film.

In 1988, Rudd, Brooke, and I left for London where I taught my final semester for Cal Poly and took early retirement. When we returned, it was to our home in Arlington, Virginia, and in the following year, 1989, we received the sad news of Mr. Beckman's death. We remained in touch with John Jr. and Louise, of course, and on June 1, 1991, we reunited with them at the wedding of our nephew, Jared Smith to Diane Chambers in San Francisco, where Rob and Joan Smith (Jared's parents) and my sister, Norma, and her husband Lou Petersen, also gathered. It was hard to imagine all the changes our lives had gone through since John, Rob, and I were eighteen years old and in the Navy in the 1940s.

In January of 1995, our daughter Brooke, who had taken up residence in California permanently, married Dr. David Goldstein in Pasadena, and John and Louise Beckman came down from Vancouver, Washington, for that occasion. Naturally, they were treated as part of our family, being the only non-relatives invited back to the house after the ceremony. Then, in June 1995, Rudd and I bought Brooke's home in Arcadia, and moved back to California. In July, John and Louise came down for his 50th reunion at North Hollywood High School, and we all got together on several occasions, one being a delightful day out at Catalina Island with Grant Taylor where we talked with Patricia Anne Moore and Bill Delbart about John's father's work and revisited the Avalon Theatre and Casino, and the other when we spent a morning listening to Ross Bellah, art director at Columbia Pictures for over fifty-four years, reminisce in his home about his long association with Mr. Beckman.

I was struck by Mr. Bellah's close resemblance to Mr. Beckman. Both were tall, elegant, slim gentlemen, amiable and modest in demeanor. Stretched out in chairs, they looked like angular afghan hounds holding their listeners spellbound—quiet, spare talkers. One listened closely as they spun tales of the dreams they wove in films. Like Mr. Beckman and John Jr., Ross Bellah was greatly impressed by *Lost Horizon* especially and the creation of Shangri-La. John Jr. remembers seeing it as a maquette first, and then watching it being realized on the Columbia ranch where it remained for a long time. "John did it all," said Ross Bellah. "I was there. I was in the room. I saw what was going on. The other fellow got the credit, but John did it all. He created Shangri-La and all the sets out of his own imagination, He should have gotten the Academy Award for it." Always, when asked which of his films he was proudest of, Mr. Beckman would answer without any hesitation, "*Lost Horizon.*"

Ross Bellah's home in Studio City is a little wonder in itself. There are two houses in a dark wood, rustic Japanese style set in a spacious yard landscaped around an old tree and a fishpond. The house was designed and built by Bellah himself in 1934. "I paid $250 for the lot," he said, "and then built this house to my own liking." In 1939, he, along with his five brothers and sisters, inherited a small amount of money from his father's estate. "I took that $3,500 and built the other house with that money," he said. The effect of his comfortable home and garden is one of peace and tranquillity—a gentleman's Shangri-La in the middle of Studio City.

So far as the other cottage goes, the one where Beckman lived for nine years until he died in it one night, "I couldn't rent it out for over six months after John's death. I kept thinking of him there," Bellah said.

Shortly after Beckman's death, Ross Bellah fell and broke his hip and had to be hospitalized. Now he uses a walker. "I've never been the same since," he says. When shown a list of Beckman's film and television credits, Bellah sighs: "I didn't realize John worked on so many films. I wouldn't even begin to know how many I worked on."

He spots Beckman's credits for *Cheers* and *Webster* in television and adds, chuckling: "Oh, these he probably did with one hand tied behind his back. *Cheers* was just a bar. They seldom moved out of it. That was true of *Designing Women* also, situated mostly in the Sugarbakers' house in Atlanta. Sometimes he would come on the set, switch a few props around and such, make a few changes. Like most art directors, he would drop around at two or three in the morning, just to see if everything was right. He worked right up to the end. I couldn't believe it when he was gone. I thought sure John would live to be at least one hundred and two years old."

CHAPTER 3: LOS ANGELES

The most valuable source of information for this period of Beckman's life is his son, John Jr., whose memory of these years is vivid For information about the Meyer and Holler firm, I am indebted to "Meyer and Holler," by Wesley Holler, son of the architect, whose reminiscences about the firm were presented to John and Louise Beckman by Louise Holler Craddock and forwarded to me on November 22, 2001. Other helpful written material included,

"Modernistic Style Receives Recognition in A.I.A., Architectural Honor Awards," *Southwest Builder and Contractor*, March 21, 1930, 30-32.

"China Interested: Celestials May Attend Opening of Chinese Theater," *Los Angeles Times,* November 24, 1926.

"Westwood Improvement Opens Soon," *Los Angeles Times*, September 29, 1929, PT.V, 8.

"Bank Home Completed in Hollywood," *Los Angeles Times*, July 1, 1928.

"A Second Life," by Steve Henson, *Los Angeles Times Magazine, January 25, 1987, 25, 41.*

"Grauman's Chinese Theater Ready for Opening Night," *Los Angeles Times,* Sunday, May 15, 1927.

Mann's Chinese Theater, souvenir brochure, Hollywood, California, 1992.

"Mann's Chinese Theater: Illusion at its Best, Architecture" by Aaron Betsky, *Los Angeles Times,* Thursday, November 7, 1991.

"Mann's New Chinese Theater Complex: Grand Opening," advertising supplement, *Los Angeles Times,* Thursday, November 7, 1991.

CHAPTER 4: CATALINA

Catalina Island is easily visited by boat from San Pedro or Long Beach, about an hour's ride. Helicopter visits are also available. Once on the island, there are excellent tours of both the Casino and the Avalon Theater where visitors can see both the interior and exterior murals of Beckman. For other material, the following are recommended:

The Casino, Avalon, Santa Catalina Island, California, Patricia Anne Moore, Catalina Island Museum Society, Inc., Avalon, California, 1979.

"Santa Catalina Island's Casino Building: Fact Sheet," Santa Catalina Island Company, Avalon, California, 1989.

"Four Catalina Projects Rise," *Los Angeles Times,* Sunday, April 22, 1928, PT.V, 4.

"Catalina Woman's Club," *Los Angeles Times,* Jack Smith, March 27, 1971.

"The New Theatre Building," *Catalina Islander,* Alma Overholt, December 19, 1928, Avalon, California, 1-2.

"Dance Hall Nears Completion," *Los Angeles Times,* February 24, 1929.

"Murals in Catalina's Casino Reflect Genius," *Los Angeles Times,* Alma Overholt, May 26, 1929, PT. III, 26.

"Miles of Tile," *Pasadena Star-News,* Barbara DeMarco Barrett, Friday, May 30, 1997, D1-2. (Information about Richard Keit's tile work)

"John Gabriel Beckman: A Los Angeles Art Treasure," Cultural Resources, *Los Angeles Conservancy News,* Judith Hammer, November/December, 1989.

CHAPTER 5: MAGIC IN THE MOVIES

For information about film directors, art directors, cinematographers, I considered the appraisals of their work given to me orally by both John Gabriel Beckman and Ross Bellah (in the long interview and taping I made with him July 28, 1995). For written material, I relied on the Margaret Herrick Motion Picture Library, Los Angeles, for microfilm, books, and folders. I also utilized the excellent reference materials available at the Grinnell College Library in Iowa. The following sources were especially helpful:

The Motion Picture Guide, Jay Robert Nash and Stanley Ralph Ross, Cinebooks, Inc., Chicago, 1986.

Directors/Filmmakers, Vol. II of *The International Dictionary of Film and Filmmakers*, Christopher Lyon, ed., St. James Press, Chicago & London, 1984.

Writers and Production Artists, Vol. IV of *The International Dictionary of Film and Filmmakers*, James Vinson and Greg S. Faller, eds., St. James Press, Chicago & London, 1984.

Masters of Lens and Light: A Checklist of Major Cinematographers and Their Feature Films, William Darby, The Scarecrow Press, Inc., Metuchen, New Jersey & London, 1991.

The Complete Film Directory, Ira Konnigsberg, NAL, New York, 1987.

The Film Encyclopedia, Ephraim Katz, Harper Perennial, New York, 1994.

CHAPTER 6: LOST CREDIT FOR LOST HORIZON

This chapter was the most difficult one to write, partly because of the collaborative nature of filmmaking and the problems inherent in proper accreditation for the efforts of all involved. Ross Bellah was most adamant in insisting that John Gabriel Beckman deserved credit for the sketches that resulted in the film version of Shangri-La, and Beckman himself told me that he was proudest of his work on this film. I telephoned Ross Bellah about other claims I encountered, but Bellah dismissed them all as spurious.

The second problem with this chapter is that, after viewing *Lost Horizon* several times over, I made the decision to try to describe it scne-by-scene as it might strike an art director assigned to design it, thus supplying the reader with how an art director reacts to a script. I, myself, first encountered the material in the 1930s when I read James Hilton's novel, and I saw the film in its first release. John Gabriel Beckman, incidentally, did not at all like Ross Hunter's color remake of the film in 1973 and refused to have anything to do with it.

For more information on *Lost Horizon*, I would suggest the following:

Frank Capra: The Name Above the Title, Frank Capra, The Macmillan Company, New York, 1971.

"Lost Horizon—A Timeless Journey," *American Cinematographer*, Sam Frank April, 1986, 30-39.

"On Location with Lost Horizon," California Living, *Los Angeles Herald Examiner,* Sam Frank, March 1, 1987, 3-6.

CHAPTER 7: THE STUDIOS THEN AND NOW

This chapter requires rapid reading and some skepticism because by the time you finish reading the whole picture may have changed. Motion pictures are a big, expensive business, and conglomerates are always on the outlook for interesting diversifications. But the money people have always been in charge. In the Golden Age of Movies, the creative people in Hollywood always complained about the bankers in New York who controlled the pursestrings of the film industry. Today, it is a little more global. In the lush days of Japanese prosperity, the Sony Corporation paid outlandish salaries to Americans to run their studio. Hollywood is still reeling from the tidal wave this had on the industry.

Whether you favor the old studio system or the new salad bowl vortex, the debate goes on. Here are a couple of current newspaper articles typical of what can be read daily, often in business sections of the press:

"Close-up, On What Went Right, Wrong: The Big Picture," *Los Angeles Times,* January 10, 2006, Patrick Goldstein, E1, E4.

"DreamWorks Sale Ends Wake--Up Call For Indie Films," *Los Angeles Times,* Claudia Eller and Sallie Hofmeister, A1, A30.

CHAPTER 8: MONSIEUR VERDOUX

As I did with *Lost Horizon,* I decided to go through this film scene-by-scene as it might be scanned by a prospective art director, hoping the reader would follow my lead. *Monsieur Verdoux* stirred up contradictory reactions in audiences from the very beginning, so I would not recommend reading reviews about it, but, instead, approach it as one would view all films ideally—with an open, unprejudiced mind. It was a landmark film for John Gabriel Beckman, but a far cry from Chaplin's beloved tramp character. What I would recommend, however, is Charlie Chaplin's *My Autobiography (Simon and Schuster, New York),* which he wrote in 1964, for its fascinating account of his early years in the theatre and film.

CHAPTER 9: THE WARNER BROTHERS YEARS

These were the great years of Beckman's career and the period which was easiest for me to write since I grew up with the films on which Beckman worked, and, once I was back in California again in 1983, I was able to visit Warner Brothers Studio, which is still in its Burbank location and available to guests.

A good book about the studio itself is *Inside Warner Bros. 1935-1951* by Rudolph Behlmer, Fireside/Simon and Schuster, New York, 1987.

Videotapes are also available for many of the Warner Brothers films which made it easy to review the work of Beckman and his colleagues.

CHAPTER 10: TELEVISION AND BEYOND

Luckily, John Gabriel Beckman was working on *Designing Women* in the 1980s and invited us to a taping at Warner Brothers, as described in the text. So, we were able to see him in action. Ross Bellah again was also a source of valuable insights into television, as were the contributions by John, Jr., Jane, and Louise Beckman. A videotape of Beckman's funeral supplied me with the comments of Chuck Liddell and Harry Thomason. Other written sources were,

Movies *Made for Television, The Telefeature and the Mini-Series, 1964-1986*, Alvin H. Marill, Baseline, New York, 1987.

"John Beckman at 91": A Life Designed for Success," *Los Angeles Times*, Libby Slate, Monday, March 27, 1989, PT.VI, 9.

"John Beckman: Designed Sets for 'Casablanca,' TV," Obituary, *Los Angeles Times*, Saturday, October 28, 1989, A34.

"John Beckman Obituary," *Variety*, Monday, October 30, 1989, 25.

"John Beckman Obituary," *Variety*, November 1, 1989.

INDEX